The Dopamine Dilemma

Mastering the Art of Reward for a Happier, Healthier You

April Homer

© **Copyright 2024 - All rights reserved.**

The content contained within this book may not be reproduced, duplicated, or transmitted without direct written permission from the author or the publisher.

Under no circumstances will any blame or legal responsibility be held against the publisher, or author, for any damages, reparation, or monetary loss due to the information contained within this book, either directly or indirectly.

Legal Notice:

This book is copyright protected. It is only for personal use. You cannot amend, distribute, sell, use, quote or paraphrase any part, or the content within this book, without the consent of the author or publisher.

Disclaimer Notice:

Please note the information contained within this document is for educational and entertainment purposes only. All effort has been executed to present accurate, up to date, reliable, complete information. No warranties of any kind are declared or implied. Readers acknowledge that the author is not engaged in the rendering of legal, financial, medical, or professional advice. The content within this book has been derived from various sources. Please consult a licensed professional before attempting any techniques outlined in this book.

By reading this document, the reader agrees that under no circumstances is the author responsible for any losses, direct or indirect, that are incurred as a result of the use of the information contained within this document, including, but not limited to, errors, omissions, or inaccuracies.

Table of Contents

INTRODUCTION 1

CHAPTER 1: INTRODUCTION TO THE DOPAMINE DILEMMA 5
- UNDERSTANDING THE BASICS OF DOPAMINE 6
- DOPAMINE'S ROLE IN THE BRAIN 8
- THE RELATIONSHIP BETWEEN DOPAMINE AND MOTIVATION 11
  - *Dopamine's Impact on Motivation* 11
  - *The Reward Cycle* 12
  - *Dopamine and Long-Term Satisfaction* 12
  - *Breaking and Building Habits* 13
  - *Dopamine, Social Bonds, and Drive* 13
- DOPAMINE'S INFLUENCE ON DAILY DECISIONS 14
  - *Finding Balance: Enjoying Now and Planning Ahead* 15
- KEY TAKEAWAYS 17

CHAPTER 2: HOW THE SCIENCE OF DOPAMINE WORKS 19
- NEUROTRANSMITTERS EXPLAINED 20
- DOPAMINE PATHWAYS IN THE BRAIN 23
  - *Dopamine's Supporting Cast and Decision-Making* 24
  - *Dopamine and Cravings* 25
  - *Understanding Pathways to Make Better Choices* 25
- HOW DOPAMINE INFLUENCES EMOTIONS 26
  - *Dopamine and Positive Emotions* 26
  - *Dopamine Deficiency and Emotional Downturns* 27
  - *Stress and Dopamine* 27
  - *Harnessing Dopamine for Emotional Health* 27
  - *Therapeutic Implications* 28
  - *A Balanced Approach to Emotional Well-Being* 28
- ROLE OF DOPAMINE IN REWARD AND PLEASURE 28
  - *Dopamine and Pleasure* 29
  - *Instant vs. Delayed Gratification* 29
  - *Dopamine and Habit Formation* 30
  - *Dopamine and Addiction* 30
  - *Practicing Delayed Gratification* 31

Empowering Positive Change Through Dopamine 31
KEY TAKEAWAYS 31

CHAPTER 3: DOPAMINE'S DOUBLE-EDGED SWORD 33

BENEFITS OF DOPAMINE ON PRODUCTIVITY AND ACHIEVEMENT 34
DOWNSIDES: ADDICTION AND UNHEALTHY HABITS 36
  Dopamine and the Addiction Mechanism 36
  The Lure of Instant Gratification 37
  Mental Health and Emotional Stability 37
  Social Media: A Dopamine Factory 37
  Finding Balance: How to Break the Cycle 38
  Dopamine: A Valuable Ally, Not the Enemy 39
BALANCING IMMEDIATE AND LONG-TERM REWARDS 39
REAL-LIFE EXAMPLES OF DOPAMINE'S DOUBLE-EDGED EFFECT 41
KEY TAKEAWAYS 42

CHAPTER 4: MODERN TEMPTATIONS AND DOPAMINE 45

IMPACT OF TECHNOLOGY ON DOPAMINE LEVELS 46
FAST FOOD AND INSTANT GRATIFICATION 48
CONSUMERISM AND IMPULSIVE BUYING 50
MANAGING DIGITAL DOPAMINE TRIGGERS 52
KEY TAKEAWAYS 54

CHAPTER 5: DOPAMINE AND DECISION-MAKING 57

DECISION FATIGUE AND DOPAMINE 58
RISK-TAKING BEHAVIOURS 60
COGNITIVE BIASES LINKED TO DOPAMINE 62
STRATEGIES TO IMPROVE DECISION-MAKING SKILLS 64
KEY TAKEAWAYS 65

CHAPTER 6: HABITS: THE GOOD, THE BAD, AND THE DOPAMINE 67

HOW HABITS ARE FORMED IN THE BRAIN 68
BREAKING BAD HABITS AND FORMING GOOD ONES 71
ROLE OF REINFORCEMENT IN HABIT LOOPS 74
CASE STUDY OF SUCCESSFUL HABIT CHANGE 76
KEY TAKEAWAYS 78

CHAPTER 7: PRACTICAL TECHNIQUES FOR BETTER CHOICES 79

DELAYING GRATIFICATION EFFECTIVELY 80
CREATING A REWARDING ENVIRONMENT 84
  Designing Your Physical Space 84

Positive Reinforcement 85
Harnessing Technology 85
Surrounding Yourself with Positivity 86
Visualising Success 86
MINDFULNESS AND SELF-AWARENESS PRACTICES 86
The Power of Meditation 87
Daily Journaling as Reflection 87
Identifying Triggers 87
Controlled Breathing Techniques 88
Building Awareness Over Time 88
BUILDING STRONGER WILLPOWER 88
The Importance of Consistency and Gradual Progression 89
Setting Clear Goals 90
The Role of Self-Reflection 90
Practising Self-Compassion 91
The Journey of Willpower Development 92

CHAPTER 8: HARNESSING DOPAMINE FOR POSITIVE GOALS 95

SETTING AND ACHIEVING SHORT-TERM GOALS 97
MAINTAINING LONG-TERM MOTIVATION 98
USING DOPAMINE TO BOOST PRODUCTIVITY 100
KEY TAKEAWAYS 101

CHAPTER 9: REAL-LIFE SUCCESS STORIES 103

ENTREPRENEURIAL SUCCESS DRIVEN BY DOPAMINE CONTROL 104
HEALTH TRANSFORMATIONS THROUGH BALANCED DOPAMINE MANAGEMENT . 106
REVERSING ADDICTIONS WITH DOPAMINE UNDERSTANDING 109
ACADEMIC ACHIEVEMENTS THROUGH DISCIPLINED DOPAMINE USE 111
KEY TAKEAWAYS 113

CHAPTER 10: MANAGING DOPAMINE: CRAFTING A BALANCED LIFE 115

CREATING HEALTHY HABITS 116
THE "DOPAMINE-FRIENDLY DAY PLANNER" 121

CONCLUSION 125

REFERENCES 131

Introduction

Imagine you are at a conference, and your eye catches trays of tempting treats. Some have fresh, juicy fruit, but right beside them are bowls brimming with cakes, cookies, and chocolates. You know the fruit is the healthier choice, but those cookies are calling out to you with a tempting allure that is hard to ignore. Why does it feel like a struggle? It is not just their sweetness; it is your brain getting overly excited, nudging you toward the sugary option. Welcome to what I call the "dopamine dilemma."

So, what exactly is this dopamine dilemma? Think of dopamine as that friend who is always ready for a good time, encouraging you to dive into whatever feels great at the moment—even if it is not the best for you long-term. Dopamine is a powerful brain chemical responsible for pleasure, motivation, and reward-seeking behaviour. It is why we reach for comfort food after a stressful day or settle into an evening of binge-watching instead of tackling that to-do list. Though dopamine's drive to keep us happy might seem helpful, it often pushes us toward instant gratification instead of more meaningful, lasting rewards.

Why does this matter? Understanding dopamine's role in decision-making can change the way we approach our choices. This is not just a scientific curiosity; it is a daily influence on everything from eating habits to productivity, even in relationships. Awareness of dopamine's impact empowers us to make decisions aligned with our goals and values, rather than falling into the loop of quick fixes that often lead to guilt and regret.

Think of dopamine as your brain's internal cheerleader, rallying you toward joy and pleasure. Yet, while dopamine can be a great motivator, it also has a sneaky side that can lead you down paths you did not plan to take. If you are thinking, "This all sounds very science-y," do not worry! We will be exploring dopamine's influence in a way that is approachable and engaging—no dense biology lessons here.

So, how does dopamine actually work? Imagine it as a built-in reward system that goes into action whenever you do something pleasurable. Eating a chocolate chip cookie, getting a compliment, or achieving a goal triggers dopamine release, creating a sense of satisfaction and encouraging you to repeat the action. Sounds simple, right? But there is a twist: not all dopamine-triggering activities are equal. While some—like exercise—benefit your well-being, others—such as mindlessly snacking on junk food—can create unhealthy habits over time.

In this book, we will dive deep into dopamine's influence on our lives, unpacking how it works and how it often leads us astray. You will gain practical tools to help you navigate moments of temptation, arming you with the knowledge to make confident, healthy choices. Together, we will explore strategies to regain control over impulsive decisions and cultivate habits that genuinely benefit you in the long run.

Beyond understanding the science behind your habits and behaviours, you will find relatable stories and real-life examples that make these concepts easy to grasp. Think of this book as your ultimate guide to mastering decision-making in a world full of distractions and dopamine temptations.

As you read, reflect on your own "dopamine dilemmas." Which choices have steered you off course, and which have helped you grow? Relating these insights to your own experiences will make this journey more relevant and impactful.

Imagine a life where impulsive choices no longer have the upper hand—a life where you can resist the urge for that extra slice of cake or the endless pull of social media. Picture yourself confidently making decisions that nourish your body and mind, leading to a sense of balanced happiness and genuine fulfilment. That is the goal of this book: to help you achieve that level of control and satisfaction.

Whether you are here for personal growth, are passionate about mental health, or work in education or healthcare, the insights in these pages will provide tools for you and others. Everyone has their own battles with dopamine, and the knowledge you will gain from this book can benefit people from all walks of life.

So, find a cosy spot (maybe with a healthy snack in hand) and get ready to embark on this journey. Here's to better choices, deeper insights, and a life that aligns with our truest values and desires.

Chapter 1:

Introduction to the Dopamine Dilemma

It is 11 p.m. on a Tuesday. You have a big presentation tomorrow and you know you should be getting some rest. Yet here you are, thumb hovering over your phone screen, debating whether to watch just one more episode of that addictive show you have been binging.

"I will regret this in the morning," you think. Yet somehow, your finger taps "Next Episode" anyway. Sound familiar? Welcome to the dopamine dilemma.

At that moment, your brain was like a battlefield. In one corner: the rational you, well aware of the importance of getting enough sleep. On the other: dopamine, that sneaky neurotransmitter, whispering promises of just a little more pleasure.

Dopamine often packs quite a punch, but do not be too quick to villainise it. That same dopamine-fuelled impulse that keeps you up too late binge-watching is also what motivates you to get out of bed for an early morning run or powers you through a tough work project. It is your brain's way of signalling what is worth your attention.

Sometimes, our internal dopamine cheerleader gets a bit too enthusiastic, leading us down paths that feel good at the moment but leave us groaning with regret later. It is often the culprit in the classic battle of instant gratification versus long-term well-being.

So how do we make peace with our dopamine-driven desires without letting them run—or ruin—our lives? We are about to unravel the mystery of this powerful brain chemical and learn how to work with it, not against it. By the end of this chapter, you will be better equipped to navigate the choppy waters of decision-making, striking a balance between feel-good moments and long-term goals. It is time to decode the dopamine dilemma.

Understanding the Basics of Dopamine

Dopamine—it is not just the latest buzzword that makes you sound smart at parties. This little neurotransmitter packs a powerful punch in how our brains operate, influencing everything from basic motor control to the thrill of winning a game. Picture your brain's communication network as a bustling city, with dopamine acting like a speedy bike messenger delivering critical messages to various regions. Without it, everything grinds to a halt; with it, actions and reactions flow smoothly.

We often think of dopamine as just the "feel-good" neurotransmitter. While it does play a role in pleasure and reward, that is only scratching the surface. Dopamine's functions extend far beyond making us happy. It helps regulate movement, attention, learning, and emotional responses—essentially a multitasking maestro orchestrating several sections of the brain's orchestra at once.

Many people assume that whenever they feel good—after a workout, eating chocolate, or getting likes on social media—it is all thanks to a flood of dopamine. While there is some truth to this, dopamine also drives behaviours like staying alert during mundane tasks or managing stress.

Attributing addiction or compulsive behaviour solely to dopamine oversimplifies a complex issue. Think of it like blaming a car crash entirely on icy roads while ignoring that the driver was texting. In cases of addiction, dopamine signals the brain that a high-reward activity (like taking drugs) is more valuable than other healthy activities. However, chemical and environmental factors also play a role.

Why is it essential to understand dopamine's role? Imagine knowing a bit about how your car works—you are less likely to panic when something goes wrong under the bonnet. Similarly, understanding how dopamine influences your motivations and choices can help you make life decisions with greater clarity.

This knowledge can improve your quality of life. It helps you recognise patterns in your behaviour, set realistic goals, and find healthier ways to seek rewards. Knowing that dopamine is not just about pleasure but also survival can reshape how you approach challenges and setbacks.

When facing daily temptations—whether it is reaching for that second slice of cake or procrastinating on an important project—understanding the mechanics of dopamine can help you make better choices. You will see these temptations as short-term urges that might bring immediate satisfaction but can sidetrack you from your long-term goals.

If you are struggling with motivation, recognising dopamine's role can be incredibly empowering. You will start to understand why some tasks feel effortless while others are hard to start. Armed with this knowledge, you can experiment with ways to trigger dopamine release constructively, like breaking larger tasks into smaller, manageable chunks or rewarding yourself for milestones achieved.

Dopamine's Role in the Brain

Let's return to the concept of the brain as a bustling city, with dopamine as one of its busiest messengers, darting around carrying vital information. Let us dive deeper into how this fascinating neurotransmitter operates and influences our daily decisions.

First up is the striatum. This area of the brain may sound like something out of a sci-fi movie, but it is actually our brain's reward hub. When you eat a delicious slice of pizza, hear your favourite song, or receive a compliment, the striatum lights up with activity. It is heavily involved in processing rewards and making us feel good about positive outcomes. When it comes to decision-making, the striatum plays a major role in whether we go for that second piece of cake or stick to our diet plan.

Dopamine affects many brain functions, ranging from movement to cognitive processing. Not only does it contribute to feelings of reward, but it also helps control movement. You can perform complex actions like typing an email or dancing because dopamine is working behind the scenes. It is like an ultimate multitasker, seamlessly switching roles to keep us moving and thinking smoothly.

Knowing that dopamine has such diverse functions can help you understand its impact on your daily life. For example, when you are deciding whether to hit the gym after a long day at work, dopamine is weighing in. Your brain remembers the post-workout endorphin rush and uses that memory to influence your choice. But if the sofa and TV call louder than the treadmill, that is dopamine too, nudging you toward the immediate pleasure of relaxation.

Individual differences in dopamine levels mean unique responses to the same situation. One person might find immense joy in running marathons, while another dreads the thought of jogging. Understanding this can help us be more compassionate toward ourselves and others in forming habits and making decisions.

Dopamine's influence also extends to motivation and goal-directed behaviour. Think about that project you have been meaning to start or a skill you have wanted to learn. Dopamine is the cheerleader in your brain, encouraging you to take that first step. As you make progress—even small wins—dopamine reinforces that behaviour, making you more likely to continue.

But dopamine is not just about instant gratification; it is also involved in anticipation and the pursuit of rewards. This explains why planning a holiday can sometimes be as enjoyable as the trip itself. Your brain releases dopamine not just when you achieve goals, but also while you are working toward them. This is why many people find joy in the process of learning or creating, not only in the final product.

Understanding dopamine's role also sheds light on why some habits are hard to break. Whether it is binge-watching your favourite show, scrolling through social media, or indulging in comfort food, these activities trigger dopamine release. Over time, your brain learns to associate these behaviours with pleasure, making them difficult to resist. The good news? You can use this knowledge to your advantage by creating new, healthier habits and sticking with them long enough for your brain to associate them with rewards, effectively reshaping your dopamine pathways.

It is important to note that while dopamine is often called the "feel-good" neurotransmitter, it is more about drive and motivation than happiness. This is why achieving a goal may not bring lasting satisfaction—your brain quickly moves on to the next objective. Recognising this can help you appreciate the journey and find contentment in the present moment, rather than always chasing the next dopamine hit.

Dopamine also plays a role in social interactions. Positive social experiences, like laughing with friends or receiving a thoughtful text, prompt dopamine release, reinforcing social bonding and encouraging us to seek out more of these interactions. This is part of why humans are so social—our brains are wired to find social connections rewarding.

So, we have touched on the striatum, dopamine's multifaceted nature, and its effects on motivation, habits, and social interactions. But what does this mean for everyday life? Knowing how these processes work can help you make more informed choices. For instance, if you know your brain craves a dopamine hit from social media, you can set boundaries to avoid getting sucked into endless scrolling, like turning off notifications or setting specific times for checking feeds.

Similarly, understanding dopamine's role in habit formation can help you build better routines. Instead of relying solely on willpower, create an environment that supports your goals. For example, keeping healthy snacks visible if you are working on your diet, or leaving workout clothes by your bed if you want to exercise in the morning.

While dopamine is powerful, it is just one piece of the complex puzzle that is your brain. By understanding its role, you can work with your brain's natural tendencies, leading to more informed decisions and a greater sense of control over your actions and habits.

The Relationship Between Dopamine and Motivation

Dopamine is more than a neurotransmitter; it is like an engine that drives our motivation, influencing decisions we make daily, whether big or small. Imagine dopamine as the backstage crew in a theatre production—hidden but integral to making the whole performance happen.

Dopamine's Impact on Motivation

Let us say you are scrolling on social media and see a delicious chocolate lava cake. Suddenly, you are craving dessert! That is dopamine in action, creating anticipation and desire, sparking motivation to seek out pleasure. But dopamine does not judge. It is as likely to urge you toward the gym as it is to keep you glued to the sofa binge-watching Netflix. The environment and cues around you guide dopamine's influence on your choices, making it adaptable to your surroundings.

Take, for example, eating healthier. If your fridge is stocked with fresh fruits and veggies and you have a friend cheering you on, dopamine will likely steer you toward healthy choices. In an environment filled with fast-food ads, however, dopamine might push you in the opposite direction. Recognising this pattern is powerful. By cultivating an environment that aligns with our goals, we can steer our dopamine-driven impulses in a beneficial direction.

The Reward Cycle

Dopamine thrives on the satisfaction of achievement. That rush you feel when you cross something off your to-do list. That is dopamine celebrating a win, encouraging you to seek that feeling again. This cycle works wonders for productivity. The first few times you drag yourself to the gym may feel tough, but over time, your brain learns to connect workouts with the dopamine boost afterwards, making it easier to look forward to exercising.

However, dopamine's reward system can sometimes lead us down risky paths. Activities like gambling deliver a high dopamine release, tempting people to chase that thrill again and again, often overlooking the risks involved. It is like putting on rose-coloured glasses—dopamine amplifies the promise of winning, blurring the reality of potential loss.

Dopamine and Long-Term Satisfaction

One of dopamine's quirks is its fondness for short-term pleasure over long-term satisfaction. Knowing this, you can take a step back before diving into an activity. Is it aligned with your bigger goals or just an immediate dopamine craving? Much like a buffet where you balance indulgence with nutritious choices, you can find balance by being mindful of your choices.

When you recognise the cues behind your impulses, you can start managing them. For example, if you are easily distracted by phone notifications, try turning them off or designating specific times to check. Building better habits becomes less about resisting and more about being proactive.

Breaking and Building Habits

Many difficult-to-break habits stem from dopamine rewards. Whether it is checking social media or indulging in comfort food, these activities release dopamine, making them hard to resist. But understanding this opens up opportunities. You can consciously create and stick to new habits, giving your brain time to associate healthier activities with rewards. For instance, starting a morning workout might feel tough at first, but after a few weeks, your brain will begin to associate exercise with positive feelings, eventually turning it into something you look forward to.

Dopamine, Social Bonds, and Drive

Dopamine also strengthens our social interactions. Laughing with friends or receiving a thoughtful message releases dopamine, reinforcing bonds and encouraging us to seek more meaningful connections. This social aspect of dopamine highlights how deeply we are wired to find relationships rewarding.

And while dopamine often carries the nickname "feel-good" neurotransmitter, it is more about motivation and drive than lasting happiness. Achieving a goal might bring a quick dopamine boost, but our brain soon moves on, pushing us toward the next target. Appreciating this can help us savour the journey itself, finding joy in the process rather than in fleeting dopamine hits.

By understanding dopamine's role, we can align with our brain's natural tendencies, making balanced, intentional choices and harnessing dopamine's power to achieve lasting fulfilment. It is not about denying pleasure but about consciously creating a balanced life, enjoying each moment while working toward goals that bring true satisfaction.

Dopamine's Influence on Daily Decisions

Picture this: You are standing in front of your fridge late at night, debating whether to grab a healthy snack or that leftover slice of pizza. Even this seemingly simple choice is shaped by dopamine. Just thinking about the pizza causes a dopamine release, sparking a rush of pleasure. This immediate response can often override thoughts about calories or long-term health goals.

Or think about the last time you instinctively picked up your phone in the middle of work and suddenly found yourself scrolling through Instagram. That is your brain searching for a quick feel-good boost, like a child sneaking sweets. These small habits add up: You know you should go to the gym, but the sofa and Netflix are calling your name. Your brain says, "This will feel great right now!" even though you know exercise would benefit you more in the long run.

These short-term pleasures can sometimes disrupt our bigger plans. Imagine you are saving for an amazing holiday, but a sale notification from your favourite shop pops up. Suddenly, you are tempted to splurge on things you do not really need. Your brain is excited by the thought of buying something new, even though that holiday would likely bring more happiness.

But there is good news—dopamine can also help you build positive habits. Say you decide to cook a healthy meal instead of ordering pizza. You not only feel proud but also physically better. Next time, your brain might actually nudge you to cook again, remembering how good it felt.

The key is recognising these patterns. Next time you reach for your phone or that bag of crisps, pause for a second and ask, "Is this really what I want to be doing right now?" It is not about denying yourself; it is about making choices that feel good now and support your goals later.

Small changes make a big difference over time. Try turning off some notifications or keeping a book nearby when you are tempted to scroll. Cook one extra meal at home each week or take a short walk when you feel the urge to binge-watch.

By understanding how dopamine influences your actions, you can start making choices that truly bring happiness and satisfaction in the long run. It is like being the boss of your own brain!

Finding Balance: Enjoying Now and Planning Ahead

Finding harmony between enjoying life's little pleasures and working toward your bigger dreams is a key part of creating a fulfilling, balanced life. It is all about understanding how dopamine—our brain's reward system—works, and then using it to support both short-term enjoyment and long-term success. By tuning into the ways dopamine can lead you to unproductive behaviours, you can make conscious choices that satisfy your immediate needs without veering off course from your ultimate goals.

To strike this balance, here are some practical steps:

1. **Identify Your Triggers:** Begin by paying attention to what drives your cravings for instant gratification. Is it stress, boredom, fatigue, or even certain social settings? Understanding your personal triggers helps you prepare and manage them before they pull you into less

productive activities. By identifying these underlying drivers, you can develop better coping mechanisms and redirect your energy toward more constructive pursuits.

2. **Set Small, Achievable Goals:** Break your long-term objectives into smaller, more manageable steps that bring consistent satisfaction and momentum. When you reach these mini milestones, your brain rewards you with dopamine, keeping you motivated to continue toward your larger ambitions. For instance, if your goal is to improve physical fitness, start with daily 10-minute exercise sessions rather than overwhelming yourself with longer, demanding workouts. Each small victory reinforces the habit, offering short-term rewards that align with long-term success.

3. **Replace Unproductive Habits with Healthy Alternatives:** Identify habits that do not serve you and gradually replace them with activities that satisfy similar needs in a healthier way. If you often find yourself mindlessly scrolling through your phone, consider replacing this habit with a fulfilling hobby, like reading, drawing, or even learning a new skill. These activities not only offer immediate satisfaction but also contribute to your personal growth and well-being over time.

By adopting these strategies, you create a balanced approach to pleasure and productivity—one that lets you enjoy life's rewards while staying committed to what truly matters to you.

Key Takeaways

- Dopamine is more than just a "feel-good" chemical; it plays a complex role in influencing our choices and behaviours.

- Dopamine impacts various aspects of life, from social media usage to motivation for exercise.

- Understanding dopamine's influence can help in managing cravings and establishing healthy boundaries.

- Recognising personal dopamine triggers allows for smarter, more intentional decision-making.

- Knowing how dopamine affects you can support the formation of healthier, more beneficial habits.

- Replace unfulfilling activities (like excessive phone use) with more rewarding hobbies.

- It is important to balance immediate gratification with long-term goals.

- Understanding dopamine can be used as a tool for personal growth and improvement.

Chapter 2:

How the Science of Dopamine Works

As the sun dipped below the horizon, casting long shadows across her living room, Emma found herself in a familiar Friday night predicament. The soft glow of her TV illuminated her face as she absent-mindedly scrolled through her Netflix queue, the remote dangling lazily from her fingers.

Suddenly, her phone buzzed, its screen lighting up with a message from her friends. "Drinks at The Rose & Crown? We are heading out now!" The words danced before her eyes, presenting an unexpected fork in her evening.

Emma's thumb hovered indecisively between the allure of *The Great British Bake Off* and the tempting promise of social interaction. Little did she know, deep within the recesses of her brain, a flurry of activity was taking place.

Dopamine, the unsung hero of decision-making, sprang into action. Like a mischievous sprite, it began painting vivid images in Emma's mind: the clinking of glasses, bursts of laughter from her friends, and the warm ambience of her favourite bar. It did not stop there; with equal enthusiasm, it conjured up images of cosy contentment—snuggling deeper into her sofa, lost in the drama of perfectly baked scones and collapsing soufflés.

As Emma weighed her options, dopamine worked its subtle magic, making both choices shimmer with possibility. After a moment's hesitation, she made her decision. Putting down the remote, she reached for her coat.

Stepping out into the crisp evening air, Emma felt a subtle thrill of excitement. Dopamine, ever the cheerleader, gave her a metaphorical pat on the back for choosing social interaction over solitary screen time.

Hours later, amid the warm glow of The Rose & Crown, Emma found herself at another crossroads. The night was winding down, and she was torn between calling it a night or staying for "just one more drink." Once again, dopamine piped up, highlighting the potential joy of extending the evening while hinting at the satisfaction of a good night's sleep.

As Emma navigated this constant negotiation between immediate pleasure and long-term satisfaction, she was unknowingly experiencing the intricate dance of neurotransmitters in her brain. Every choice she made, from the monumental to the mundane, had a dash of dopamine guiding her through the complex web of decisions that shaped her daily life.

Neurotransmitters Explained

Neurotransmitters are like the brain's own version of text messages, zipping around to deliver crucial information from one neuron to another. Picture them as tiny dispatchers, diligently circulating updates to keep everything running smoothly.

Dopamine, however, stands out with its VIP status in the brain's complex chemical network. Think of it as your brain's personal DJ, spinning tracks that not only make you feel good but also guide your decisions—whether to let loose and dance like no one is watching or politely decline and return to your seat.

Dopamine is part of a crew of neurotransmitters, each with its own unique role. Some keep you relaxed, while others give you a surge of excitement. The brain is like a bustling city, and neurotransmitters are its traffic directors, keeping things flowing smoothly without major crashes—or existential crises.

Maintaining a balance between neurotransmitters is a bit like juggling flaming torches—without the fire hazards. When they are in harmony, life feels balanced. But when the scales tip too far, you may feel off-kilter, anxious, or blue. It is like your brain saying, "Oops! Dial that back a notch, please!"

Dopamine can be compared to a hyper-efficient postal worker darting between neurons, delivering signals that shape how we feel and decide. But its journey is not always straightforward. It winds through a convoluted maze of pathways, influencing how we perceive rewards and make choices, which might explain why late-night snacks or rewatching a favourite show sometimes seem so much more appealing than that to-do list.

Imagine your brain as a massive theme park, with different areas dedicated to various functions. Dopamine is that one thrill ride everyone wants to try—it is exhilarating, keeps you coming back, and operates areas like the "Reward Zone," "Motivation Mountain," and "Decision-Making Donut Shack."

In the "Reward Zone," dopamine plays mascot, high fiving you every time you accomplish something. Finished a tough workout? High-five! Completed a big project? Double high-five! This positive reinforcement explains why achieving even small goals feels so good.

At "Motivation Mountain," dopamine is the enthusiastic tour guide, constantly pointing out exciting new peaks to climb, encouraging you to push forward even when the path gets steep. Without it, Motivation Mountain would feel like a molehill, making it hard to tackle new challenges or pursue your dreams.

The "Decision-Making Donut Shack" is where things get interesting. Here, dopamine serves as both race announcer and fuel, revving up your engine when you face choices—especially those with rewards. Should you have that extra slice of pizza? Dopamine might be cheering, "Go for it!" But it is not all about instant gratification; dopamine also helps you weigh long-term benefits, nudging you to choose the salad in favour of better health down the road.

Dopamine also has a sneaky side. Like that friend who convinces you to go out on a Tuesday despite an early meeting, dopamine whispers, "Just one more episode," when binge-watching at 2 a.m., or nudges you to check your phone yet again, hoping for that little thrill of a new notification.

But dopamine is not trying to lead you astray; it is doing its job, keeping you engaged and helping you seek out beneficial experiences. The trick is to work with your dopamine system, not against it.

Think of it like training a puppy. Instead of scolding a puppy for being excited about everything, you channel that energy into positive behaviours. Similarly, you can guide your dopamine-driven impulses into productive activities. Enjoy the rush of completing tasks? Break big projects into smaller steps to savour more frequent dopamine boosts. Addicted to social media? Channel that enthusiasm into real-life social interactions.

Understanding dopamine's role also helps explain why breaking habits is challenging. That daily chocolate bar is not just a snack—it is a dopamine party in your brain. Skipping it leaves your brain asking, "Where is the party?" Replacing habits, rather than simply quitting them, lets you redirect dopamine's flow, creating new pathways for that reward-seeking energy.

So next time you are making a decision—choosing lunch, starting a new hobby, or just unwinding—remember the complex dance of neurotransmitters in your brain. Dopamine is there, playing its part in this intricate ballet, guiding choices and colouring experiences.

Awareness of this process can help you make more conscious decisions. Pause and ask, "Is this my genuine desire, or dopamine chasing a quick reward?" This awareness will not always lead to perfect choices—sometimes that late-night ice cream is totally worth it—but it will lead to more informed ones.

In the end, dopamine is not good or bad; it is a tool your brain uses to navigate the world. Learning to work with it, rather than being unconsciously driven by it, can bring a more balanced and fulfilling life.

Dopamine Pathways in the Brain

Dopamine pathways are central to understanding how pleasure, reward, and movement coordination work in the brain. Let us break down the two most influential ones: the mesolimbic and nigrostriatal pathways. Think of them as dopamine's main highways, each with a specific purpose.

1. **The Mesolimbic Pathway:** This is dopamine's "feel-good" expressway, running from the ventral tegmental area (VTA) to the nucleus accumbens. If you have ever felt a surge of happiness from a delicious treat or the thrill of completing a game level, the mesolimbic pathway is behind it. This pathway rewards pleasurable experiences, encouraging us to repeat actions that bring enjoyment. It is a primary driver of motivation and reward-seeking, essentially our brain's way of saying, "That felt great—do it again!"

2. **The Nigrostriatal Pathway:** This pathway is dopamine's route for coordinating smooth, controlled movement. It runs from the substantia nigra to the striatum, acting like a choreographer for our motor skills. Without it, simple actions like reaching for a glass of water or walking smoothly would become clumsy or even impossible. When dopamine levels are disrupted in this pathway, it can lead to conditions like Parkinson's disease, where smooth movement control becomes impaired.

Dopamine's Supporting Cast and Decision-Making

Dopamine is not the sole player in the brain's decision-making orchestra—it collaborates with other neurotransmitters like serotonin, GABA, and glutamate to create a balanced environment that guides our choices. Imagine dopamine as the spark, pushing you toward that last slice of pizza or one more episode in a binge. Meanwhile, serotonin influences your mood, bringing in a touch of satisfaction or restraint, while GABA promotes a calming effect, allowing you to step back and assess the situation without acting impulsively. Conversely, glutamate strengthens connections in the brain, supporting memory and learning so you can recall past decisions and make better choices. Together, this team creates a well-rounded brain network that helps you weigh options, control urges, and make decisions that balance short-term satisfaction with long-term benefits. This collaboration of neurotransmitters ultimately shapes how we experience and act on our cravings and desires.

Dopamine and Cravings

Dopamine's role in cravings and addiction reveals the double-edged nature of this influential neurotransmitter. Known for encouraging the repetition of rewarding experiences, dopamine motivates us to pursue activities that bring us joy or satisfaction, reinforcing behaviours that lead to pleasurable outcomes. But this system can be exploited, especially when substances like drugs come into play. These substances hijack dopamine pathways, creating a "pseudo-reward" by artificially boosting dopamine levels. This trickery leads the brain to prioritise the substance, reinforcing the behaviour even if it is harmful, as if an overbearing guest overstays their welcome, urging everyone to keep partying when it is long past time to wind down. This is why certain habits, especially those tied to substance use, can be so difficult to break—they are rooted in a misdirected dopamine response that our brain misinterprets as essential.

Understanding Pathways to Make Better Choices

Gaining insight into how dopamine pathways function can be like discovering a treasure map of the mind, revealing why specific behaviours feel irresistibly rewarding, whether they are beneficial or detrimental. These invisible circuits play a critical role in shaping our motivations and guiding our responses, explaining why some impulses can feel so compelling. When we understand how these pathways work, we are better equipped to make conscious choices, navigating dopamine's influence with intention rather than being swayed by it. This knowledge empowers us to align our behaviours with our personal goals, leveraging dopamine's power to reinforce positive habits while resisting its pull toward choices that may not serve us well in the long run.

How Dopamine Influences Emotions

Dopamine, often called the brain's "feel-good" neurotransmitter, plays an essential role in shaping our emotional landscape. It is like having an internal DJ that selects mood-boosting tunes when we engage in activities that please us. Beyond simply creating moments of joy, dopamine also contributes to emotional stability, reinforcing the actions and experiences that promote positive feelings. It guides us in choosing behaviours that lead to enjoyment, rewarding us for these actions with a sense of well-being and satisfaction.

Dopamine and Positive Emotions

Imagine hearing your favourite song—the one that instantly lifts your mood. When we engage in activities we enjoy, dopamine is released into specific areas of the brain, creating a positive feedback loop. This dopamine release not only makes us feel good at the moment but also increases the likelihood that we will seek out similar experiences in the future. It is the brain's way of giving us a "gold star," celebrating the decision to engage in something enjoyable and encouraging us to repeat it. This reward mechanism is at the core of why we pursue activities that make us feel good, from spending time with loved ones to indulging in hobbies and passions.

Dopamine Deficiency and Emotional Downturns

When dopamine levels are low, it is like the brain's reward system loses its sparkle, leading to a drop in mood and motivation. Life may begin to feel grey and unmotivating, and even simple tasks can start to seem overwhelming. Low dopamine levels disrupt this positive reinforcement system, which is closely linked to negative emotional states. Without sufficient dopamine, decisions become harder, and day-to-day actions can feel like a struggle. Chronic dopamine deficiencies are associated with conditions such as major depressive disorder (MDD) and Parkinson's disease, emphasizing the critical role dopamine plays in maintaining emotional health and resilience (Belujon & Grace, 2017).

Stress and Dopamine

Stress acts as a chaotic influence on dopamine levels, distorting our emotional responses and muddling our decision-making processes. In stressful situations, dopamine production can be disrupted, leading to imbalances that make it harder to handle emotions effectively. This shift can cause us to make impulsive choices or avoid necessary changes, often increasing feelings of frustration, irritability, or anxiety. Prolonged stress can deplete dopamine reserves, leaving us with less resilience to cope with challenges and potentially amplifying negative emotional states.

Harnessing Dopamine for Emotional Health

Understanding dopamine's role in our emotional well-being offers us powerful tools to improve our mood and maintain emotional stability. Regular activities like exercise, listening to uplifting music, or engaging in favourite hobbies stimulate dopamine production naturally, helping to boost positive emotions. Additionally, managing stress through practices like meditation, deep breathing, or mindfulness can prevent dopamine depletion, supporting a more balanced emotional state. These activities can help us build resilience and increase our capacity to manage difficult situations with a more balanced outlook.

Therapeutic Implications

Due to dopamine's significant impact on mood, treatments for emotional disorders frequently target dopamine pathways. Certain antidepressants, for instance, are designed to increase the availability of dopamine in the brain to help alleviate symptoms of depression and improve emotional regulation. However, because brain chemistry is highly individual, the effectiveness of these treatments can vary widely from person to person, and they are often part of a broader treatment plan tailored to each individual's needs (Juárez Olguín et al., 2016).

A Balanced Approach to Emotional Well-Being

Recognising dopamine's influence on our emotions and behaviour empowers us to make informed choices that support our mental health. By adopting practices that naturally enhance dopamine levels, managing stress effectively, and, if needed, exploring therapeutic interventions, we gain valuable tools to improve mood, resilience, and overall well-being.

Role of Dopamine in Reward and Pleasure

Dopamine is central to how we experience pleasure and rewards, guiding decisions, habits, and even the ability to resist temptations. Often called the brain's "reward chemical," dopamine acts like a personal cheerleader, motivating us to repeat actions that bring enjoyment and satisfaction. It is the silent driver behind why we reach for a second slice of cake or get a thrill from hitting a personal best at the gym. Understanding dopamine's role in our brain can help us manage its influence, making it a tool for achieving balanced and meaningful satisfaction.

Dopamine and Pleasure

Each time we indulge in a pleasurable activity—whether it is savouring a favourite treat or completing a challenging workout—dopamine rewards us with a chemical boost, a surge that brings a moment of happiness or fulfilment. This boost does not just make us feel good; it also reinforces the experience, making us more likely to seek out similar activities in the future. Dopamine creates a powerful feedback loop that links positive actions with pleasure, encouraging us to re-engage with what brings us joy and creating a natural inclination to repeat these behaviours.

Instant vs. Delayed Gratification

Imagine binge-watching your favourite show while a looming deadline for work waits in the background. The pull of dopamine makes that next episode feel overwhelmingly tempting, nudging us toward the satisfaction of the present moment. While dopamine often drives us toward instant gratification, it is possible to redirect this pull to benefit us in the long term. By pausing and actively assessing the benefits of each option, we can start shifting toward choices that support long-term rewards, which often bring a more fulfilling sense of satisfaction. The ability to delay gratification strengthens with practice, helping us make decisions that better align with our broader goals and values.

Dopamine and Habit Formation

Dopamine is instrumental in forming habits, reinforcing actions that result in positive outcomes. Repeating activities that yield satisfaction—like exercising or eating a nutritious meal—encourages dopamine to signal the brain with a "thumbs up," marking these actions as beneficial. Over time, as we consistently perform these rewarding behaviours, dopamine strengthens the mental association between the activity and its positive outcome, turning once-intentional actions into automatic habits. This process is how small, positive behaviours gradually become integrated into our routines, shaping long-lasting habits that support our well-being.

Dopamine and Addiction

While dopamine can encourage positive habits, it also plays a significant role in addictive behaviours. Activities that produce strong dopamine surges, such as gambling or excessive gaming, create an intense reward signal in the brain, leading us to crave the activity repeatedly. This surge can overpower the brain's logical decision-making processes, making resisting cravings difficult. Over time, these dopamine-driven patterns can alter brain function, reinforcing the habit to the point where it begins to disrupt everyday life and decision-making. The power of dopamine in these cases can be so compelling that rational choices are often overshadowed, emphasising the dual nature of dopamine as both a motivator and a potential source of addiction (Volkow et al., 2010).

Practicing Delayed Gratification

When faced with a choice between immediate pleasure and a greater, future reward, taking a moment to pause can be transformative. Recognising the immediate pull of satisfaction while considering the potential benefits of delayed gratification can help rewire the brain to appreciate long-term rewards. This pause allows us to weigh our choices more thoughtfully, making it easier over time to resist impulses that do not align with our larger goals. Practising delayed gratification is a way to shift dopamine's influence, guiding it toward choices that bring sustained happiness.

Empowering Positive Change Through Dopamine

By understanding dopamine's role in reward and pleasure, we gain insight into why we crave certain behaviours and how habits form. With this knowledge, we can harness dopamine to create positive, lasting changes, encouraging healthy habits and enabling better decision-making. Recognising how dopamine impacts our daily lives can help us take control, transforming the "reward chemical" into an ally for personal growth and lasting well-being.

Key Takeaways

- Dopamine orchestrates emotions, decisions, and cravings, acting as a central guide in the brain.
- Dopamine influences both minor daily choices and major life decisions.

- Dopamine is essential in driving the brain's pleasure and reward mechanisms, motivating us toward repeated behaviours.

- Dopamine's role helps us understand why we develop certain cravings and habits.

- Knowledge of dopamine can empower us to adjust behaviours, aligning them with personal goals.

- Living with dopamine's effects is like being in a reality show, where each decision shapes outcomes.

- Awareness of dopamine's impact aids in forming positive habits and fostering growth.

- With awareness, it is possible to resist dopamine-driven urges, building healthier routines.

- Though dopamine is powerful, individuals still have control over their choices and actions.

Chapter 3:

Dopamine's Double-Edged Sword

Alex stared at his phone, thumb hovering over the "Buy Now" button for a pair of shoes he absolutely did not need. It was 2 a.m., and he had stumbled upon them during what was supposed to be a quick social media check before bed. Three hours later, here he was, contemplating his seventeenth pair of trainers.

"Just one more scroll," he muttered, echoing the mantra that had led him down this late-night shopping rabbit hole. As he debated the merits of yet another purchase, a part of his brain lit up like a Christmas tree. That was dopamine, his brain's resident party planner, tossing confetti at the mere thought of a new acquisition.

Suddenly, his alarm blared, jolting him back to reality. It was 6 a.m.—time for his morning run, a habit he had painstakingly cultivated over the past few months. As he laced up his current favourite pair of trainers (only two weeks old), he felt a different kind of excitement bubbling up. This time, dopamine was cheering him on for a healthier choice.

In the span of a few hours, Alex had experienced both sides of dopamine's influence—the temptation of immediate gratification and the satisfaction of working toward a long-term goal.

Benefits of Dopamine on Productivity and Achievement

Dopamine is a powerful motivator, propelling us toward goals and rewarding us with a sense of accomplishment along the way. You know that small thrill after ticking off a task on your to-do list? That is dopamine, giving you a quick boost of satisfaction and encouraging you to keep going.

As we engage in any task—whether it is mastering a new skill, completing a project, or working out—dopamine is released with each small step forward. This internal reward system works like a gentle push, saying, "Well done! Keep it up!" It transforms goals from daunting mountains into motivating stepping stones, making the journey itself rewarding. For instance, you might start running for health benefits, but over time, the simple act of running becomes satisfying in itself, thanks to dopamine's influence.

Higher dopamine levels also sharpen focus and engagement, almost like putting on mental blinkers. When dopamine is up, distractions fade, and your brain tunes into what you are doing with greater clarity and enthusiasm. Imagine tackling a complex puzzle or a challenging project at work; with sufficient dopamine, you are immersed in the task, deeply engaged, and achieving a sense of flow where time seems to disappear.

Beyond boosting motivation, dopamine is also a catalyst for creativity and problem-solving. Research shows that dopamine's role in various brain pathways significantly impacts cognitive flexibility and creative thinking (Zabelina et al., 2016). It enables us to shift fluidly between ideas and connect seemingly unrelated concepts. Picture those lightbulb moments when you suddenly link two ideas together in a fresh, innovative way—that is dopamine facilitating a leap in your thought process.

Dopamine's influence extends into social interactions, too. After a lively conversation or an enjoyable outing with friends, that euphoric feeling is dopamine strengthening social bonds. It promotes teamwork by fostering unity and shared purpose, which in turn boosts morale in collaborative environments. This dopamine-induced positivity encourages people to contribute openly and support each other, creating a cycle of increased collaboration and motivation.

However, dopamine is best used in balance—too much can lead to impulsivity and rash decisions. Think of dopamine like a seesaw: the right amount keeps you motivated and goal-focused, but tipping the scales too far can lead to impulsive behaviour. By understanding how dopamine works, we can harness it wisely to keep ourselves purposefully engaged without going overboard.

To make the most of dopamine's role in motivation and achievement, breaking down big tasks into smaller, manageable steps is a great strategy. Each mini milestone releases a small surge of dopamine, sustaining motivation throughout the process and preventing burnout. Incorporating creativity into your daily routine, like sketching ideas during a break or jotting down thoughts, can keep dopamine levels steady and enhance problem-solving. Regular social interactions, whether through virtual or face-to-face meetings, also stimulate dopamine, boosting both personal drive and group motivation.

By tapping into dopamine's potential thoughtfully, you can enhance your productivity, creativity, and overall satisfaction in both work and life.

Downsides: Addiction and Unhealthy Habits

Dopamine can feel like that charming friend who tempts you with "just one more" piece of cake, leading to a few more than you planned. While dopamine fuels motivation and rewards, an unchecked pursuit of it can steer us into challenging waters.

Dopamine and the Addiction Mechanism

Dopamine plays a key role in our brain's reward system, cheering us on every time we do something pleasurable. Whether it is a chocolate fix or winning a round of your favourite game, dopamine gives us that feel-good sensation. However, this reward system does not always know when to stop. If left unchecked, it can lead to compulsive behaviours. Substances like alcohol and activities like gambling are classic examples of people chasing the high dopamine delivers, spiralling into addiction. In this cycle, the brain becomes wired to crave that dopamine rush, almost like it is on autopilot toward self-destruction.

Imagine your brain as a city, with dopamine as the overenthusiastic mayor who keeps throwing parties (dopamine surges). At first, these dopamine-fuelled "parties" lift morale and keep the city thriving. But when the mayor throws parties every night, resources run thin, and the once-fun events become exhausting. This is similar to addiction—the brain becomes accustomed to high dopamine levels and requires more of it just to feel "normal."

The Lure of Instant Gratification

Dopamine can also be a troublemaker when it comes to instant gratification versus delayed rewards. Picture yourself in front of a vending machine with a choice between a quick chocolate fix or saving your money for a meal later. Dopamine nudges us toward immediate pleasure, making long-term goals feel distant and challenging to achieve. With our brains used to quick fixes, making decisions requiring patience can feel as tough as climbing a mountain without any gear.

In this sense, dopamine is like the impulsive child in class who answers before thinking. Sometimes they are right, but often taking a moment leads to better outcomes. Practices like mindfulness and meditation help us pause and reflect, giving us the patience to make choices aligned with our longer-term goals.

Mental Health and Emotional Stability

Over time, dopamine-seeking can leave us feeling empty. When we constantly chase highs—whether through social interactions, achievements, or digital content—everyday life can seem bland. It is like eating spicy food with every meal; soon, regular flavours no longer satisfy, and it takes more "spice" to get the same effect. This can elevate anxiety, increase the risk of depression, and make it hard to feel content without constant stimulation.

Social Media: A Dopamine Factory

Social media platforms like Instagram and Twitter are prime dopamine factories, designed to keep us checking our phones. Each ping or notification is a potential dopamine hit, and while a few likes or comments may seem harmless, they can easily turn into a digital addiction. These platforms use algorithms that keep us guessing, much like slot machines, making it easy to get hooked by the unpredictability of each update (McLean Hospital, 2024). Studies show that heavy social media use can harm sleep, memory, and overall mood, making users feel anxious and often leading to unfavourable comparisons with the highlight reels they see online.

Imagine social media as a giant, never-ending party. At first, it is exciting, to connect with people and share experiences. But as the party drags on, exhaustion sets in. You want to leave, but you are afraid of missing out. This is the dopamine-driven cycle that keeps us scrolling long after it has stopped being fun.

Finding Balance: How to Break the Cycle

Cutting off sources of instant gratification is not practical, but understanding dopamine's pull can help us create balance. Setting social media boundaries, for instance, is a good start. Practising "dopamine breaks"—taking time off high-stimulation activities—helps reset the brain's reward system, allowing us to rediscover satisfaction in simpler pleasures. Going for a walk, reading, or connecting with friends face-to-face provides more sustainable joy than a quick digital fix.

Building longer-term sources of dopamine is equally important. Learning a new skill, completing a project, or volunteering provides a steady, more balanced stream of dopamine that is less prone to the highs and lows of instant gratification. This way, dopamine can be used to build rewarding habits that align with larger goals.

Dopamine: A Valuable Ally, Not the Enemy

Dopamine itself is not the problem; it is how we engage with it. By setting up reward systems that align with long-term goals—such as treating yourself after a productive day—you can use dopamine to reinforce positive habits. It is about creating a lifestyle where we appreciate the journey, not just the quick dopamine hits.

So, the next time you are tempted to check your phone for the hundredth time or go for that extra slice of cake, take a moment to pause. Ask yourself if the action aligns with your larger goals and values. Mindful choices help harness dopamine for lasting fulfilment rather than momentary pleasure, creating a balanced, joyful life.

Balancing Immediate and Long-Term Rewards

Balancing immediate satisfaction with long-term goals is a challenge everyone faces—it is that classic choice between enjoying something now or holding out for a bigger reward later. Think of it like choosing between a delicious cupcake today or keeping on track to fit into your favourite jeans next month. Both options offer rewards, but in different ways and at different times.

One helpful strategy is to break down your long-term goal into smaller, rewarding milestones. This approach is like setting up a treasure hunt where each checkpoint offers a mini reward, helping to keep you motivated along the way. If your goal is to run a marathon, for example, you could celebrate each time you reach a 5km milestone. These smaller successes make the journey more enjoyable and help you stay focused on progress rather than just the end result.

Mindfulness can also be a game-changer. It is like a "pause button" that lets you step back and think before making an impulsive choice, such as binge-watching TV instead of working on a project. Taking a moment to ask yourself, "Does this choice support what I really want in the long term?" can make it easier to choose a path aligned with your goals.

Finding joy in the process, not just the outcome, can make a huge difference. When learning a new language, for instance, try to savour the discovery of each new word and the insights into a new culture, rather than focusing solely on fluency. This kind of enjoyment in the journey not only makes the process more fun but also keeps you motivated. Sometimes, visualising yourself achieving the end goal—like speaking that language fluently or crossing a marathon finish line—can help make your goal feel more tangible and inspiring.

Of course, we all have setbacks, so do not be too hard on yourself if you slip up occasionally. Just refocus and keep moving forward. Having supportive friends or mentors who can cheer you on can also make a big difference, especially when things get tough.

Balancing immediate pleasures with long-term goals does not have to be an all-or-nothing approach. By using these strategies, you can make choices that support both your current happiness and your future aspirations, setting you up for lasting satisfaction.

Real-Life Examples of Dopamine's Double-Edged Effect

Dopamine's influence on our choices can be powerful, as shown in these real-life examples of people balancing immediate rewards with long-term happiness.

Take John, who launched a small online business. He leveraged dopamine's motivating power by setting small, achievable goals, celebrating each step. Every milestone gave him a boost of satisfaction, inspiring him to keep going. It is like treating yourself to a little dessert after every healthy meal—it keeps the journey exciting and manageable.

On the flip side, Maria experienced dopamine's darker side. She became addicted to drugs; drawn by the intense rush of pleasure they provided. Over time, the temporary highs took a toll on her life and health. But Maria made a crucial change, substituting unhealthy dopamine hits with better habits like exercise and meditation. It is like swapping junk food for nutritious snacks—she still enjoys a boost, but it is healthier and more sustainable.

Then there is the Smith family, who noticed they were spending too much time in front of screens, missing out on meaningful family moments. The quick dopamine hits from watching TV and scrolling online were fun but did not offer lasting satisfaction. They decided to have tech-free evenings for games and outdoor activities, trading fast entertainment for deeper family connections. It is like choosing between a quick snack and a homemade meal shared with loved ones—one is instantly gratifying, but the other is far more fulfilling.

Sarah's story reveals the impact of social media on dopamine cravings. She enjoyed the rush from likes and comments but soon felt empty. She realised that, while social media can provide instant boosts, it does not offer the same deep satisfaction as real friendships. Spending time with a close friend felt more nourishing and joyful. It is like choosing between a quick chat online or a meaningful afternoon with a friend—both have value, but one brings more lasting happiness.

These stories highlight how dopamine can guide us in different directions. While it is natural to enjoy things that feel good right away, balancing these pleasures with activities that bring long-term happiness can lead to a more fulfilling life. By understanding dopamine's effect, we can make choices that satisfy us both now and in the future.

Key Takeaways

- Dopamine is like a two-faced friend in our brains. It can drive us to achieve or keep us stuck in unhealthy habits.

- Dopamine can keep us stuck in unhealthy habits. Activities like endless social media scrolling can give instant gratification but may detract from deeper satisfaction.

- Reduce screen time and increase face-to-face interactions. Building real connections can lead to more fulfilling dopamine boosts.

- Balance quick rewards and long-term achievements. Both can be meaningful, but finding a balance helps avoid burnout or dissatisfaction.

- Find joy in both quick wins and longer journeys. Embracing both can keep motivation strong and make the process more enjoyable.

Chapter 4:
Modern Temptations and Dopamine

Rahul stared at his phone. It was 3 a.m., and he knew he should be sleeping. Yet here he was, caught in the familiar glow of his screen, debating whether to watch just one more video. "Five more minutes," he promised himself, knowing full well it was a lie he had already told himself a dozen times that night.

Across town, his friend Josh was having a similar experience—only with online shopping. A flash sale notification had pinged his phone, and now he found himself adding items to his cart that he neither needed nor could afford. The thrill of the potential purchase was too enticing to resist.

Meanwhile, their mutual friend Lisa was hunched over her gaming console, eyes bloodshot but alert. "Just one more level," she muttered, ignoring the early morning light creeping through her blinds. She had been saying that for hours, each completed level giving her a rush that demanded encore after encore.

What Rahul, Josh, and Lisa did not realise was that they were all caught in the same trap—a dopamine-fuelled cycle of instant gratification. Their late-night activities, while different, shared a common thread: each tap, purchase, and level-up was a tiny hit of pleasure, urging them to continue despite the looming consequences of a sleepless night and an unproductive day ahead.

Impact of Technology on Dopamine Levels

In the ever-evolving digital age, technology has honed its ability to exploit our brain's natural dopamine responses. This neurotransmitter, often referred to as the "feel-good" chemical, plays a crucial role in reinforcing behaviours by rewarding us with feelings of pleasure. Technological advancements have taken advantage of this biological pathway, weaving cycles of reward and dependency into our daily routines.

Social media is a prime example of how modern platforms are engineered for maximum engagement. These platforms thrive on user interaction, using likes, shares, and comments to create mini dopamine hits that keep users coming back for more. Notifications are deliberately designed to grab your attention—whether it is a new message, a comment, or a like. This careful crafting triggers anticipation and excitement, with the anticipation itself releasing dopamine and heightening our urge to check our phones repeatedly. As users indulge in these interactions, they find themselves caught in a cycle, constantly seeking validation and engagement, which can foster dependency. Spending hours scrolling through feeds often leads to less time spent on meaningful offline activities, impacting both productivity and real-world relationships.

Video games also capitalise on our brain's reward system by offering continuous achievements and surprises that mimic real-life wins. From levelling up to unlocking rare items, each accomplishment provides a surge of dopamine, encouraging gamers to pursue further victories. For many, the immersive experience of video games offers an escape from the mundane aspects of life, luring them into a virtual realm filled with rewards. This form of entertainment can blur the line between virtual and actual accomplishments, sometimes leading individuals to prioritise gaming over everyday responsibilities.

The constant stimulation keeps dopamine levels elevated, making it challenging to disengage from the screen and focus on tasks that do not offer immediate gratification.

Our smartphones have become pocket-sized dopamine machines. The constant ping of notifications—texts, emails, and app alerts—keeps us in a loop of perpetual interaction. It is almost Pavlovian; each ding triggers an automatic response, prompting us to check what we have received. This conditioning leads to a craving for digital interaction at any moment, making it a Herculean feat to focus on sustained tasks. Research shows that even the presence of a smartphone can reduce cognitive capacity, as our brains remain partially engaged with potential digital interruptions. This phenomenon can severely impact concentration and productivity, as the brain struggles to toggle between tasks and maintain attention.

Binge-watching embodies another facet of technology's manipulation of dopamine. With streaming services providing entire seasons at our fingertips, it is all too easy to slip into marathon viewing sessions. Each cliffhanger and plot twist holds us captive, compelling us to click "next episode" for another dose of excitement. Though enjoyable, extended viewing sessions disrupt our perception of time and eat away at hours meant for other pursuits. Prolonged exposure to screens late into the night can tamper with sleep cycles, leaving viewers exhausted and less productive the following day. This habit, while offering temporary pleasure, can gradually erode time management skills and inhibit our ability to complete necessary tasks efficiently.

To maintain control over your engagement with technology, you need to recognise when enjoyment is turning into compulsion. Technology itself is not inherently harmful, but our relationship with it requires careful management to prevent unhealthy dependencies. Being mindful of how and when we interact helps us set boundaries, ensuring that the digital world enhances rather than detracts from real-life fulfilment and responsibilities.

To maintain a healthy balance, pay attention to your own experiences. Are hours slipping by unnoticed? Do you find yourself reaching for your phone during quiet moments? Building intentional habits and setting conscious limits on tech use can help you enjoy its rewards without becoming addicted.

Fast Food and Instant Gratification

Fast food culture is like that mischievous friend who always tempts you to break your diet. You know, the one who convinces you that a midnight burger run is a great idea, even though you have already had dinner. Fast food's power over us boils down to dopamine.

When you bite into a juicy burger or nibble on crispy fries, your brain rewards you by releasing dopamine, providing an immediate sense of pleasure. Sugary and high-fat foods are especially potent dopamine boosters. This quick hit of happiness reinforces cravings, making you want more with each bite. It is like a culinary joy ride that keeps pulling you back for another round. This phenomenon can lead to impulsive eating patterns, where grabbing a greasy snack becomes irresistible even when we are not hungry. The cycle spins like a never-ending carousel of munchies.

Now, add marketing strategies to the mix, and you have a recipe for indulgence that is hard to resist. Think about those mouthwatering ads showcasing glistening burgers or delightful desserts, accompanied by catchy jingles. These are not just random creations; they are meticulously designed to trigger your dopamine response. The vibrant colours and tempting visuals tap into your brain's reward system, urging you to make that impulse purchase. Whether it is a giant billboard or a short video clip on social media, these strategies know how to press the "buy" button in your brain.

Fast food has also deeply rooted itself in our social and cultural norms. Eating out at fast-food joints often becomes a shared experience, whether it is late-night snacks with friends or family meals on busy nights. Society subtly promotes these quick options, intensifying the dopamine rush through communal dining experiences. It is almost like a rite of passage—how many childhoods are marked by those first visits to a favourite fast-food chain? Sharing these moments with others adds a layer of emotional connection, further amplifying the dopamine hits associated with these meals.

So, how do we fight back against the dopamine-driven impulses that fast food cultivates? Implementing healthier eating strategies is one way to counter the allure. While it is easy to fall prey to the convenience of fast food, taking proactive steps toward balanced nutrition can help. Swapping sugary snacks for fruits or opting for home-cooked meals can gently retrain our brains to crave less addictive foods. These small changes can significantly alter our relationship with food, helping us break free from the dopamine roller coaster.

Cooking at home not only allows for control over ingredients but also turns meal preparation into a rewarding activity. Preparing a dish from scratch engages different senses, from the sound of sizzling vegetables to the aroma of fresh herbs. This process provides a slower, more sustained dopamine release, as opposed to the quick spike offered by fast food. Plus, discovering the joy of cooking and savouring homemade meals can be just as satisfying, if not more so, than the instant gratification of fast food.

Mindful eating is another powerful tactic. It involves being present and paying attention during meals, savouring each bite, and listening to your body's hunger cues. By slowing down and appreciating the textures and flavours of food, you can retrain your brain to value quality over quantity. This practice helps diminish the need for excess consumption driven by our brain's desire for that next dopamine hit.

Consumerism and Impulsive Buying

In the world of consumer culture, one of the most potent forces driving our buying behaviour is dopamine—a sneaky chemical in our brains that gets us excited and motivated. It is like our brain's little happiness delivery guy, rushing to flood our system with good vibes whenever we are on the verge of snagging that perfect pair of shoes or scoring a great deal. Here is where it gets interesting: shopping environments are designed to play with this dopamine response, using marketing tricks that make even the most disciplined shoppers think, "I did not need this, but it is so shiny and new!"

Picture yourself walking into a shop filled with tantalizing scents, catchy music, and displays that seem to whisper, "Buy me!" These elements are not just for aesthetics; they are crafted to give you a mini dopamine rush, enticing you to grab things you did not plan on buying. The thrill of the hunt, paired with attractive banners screaming "SALE!" can turn an innocent window-shopping trip into a full-blown buying spree. It is like a treasure map leading straight to unnecessary purchases.

Speaking of unnecessary purchases, online shopping has taken impulse buying to a whole new level. The ease and convenience of clicking a button to buy something mean instant gratification has never been more accessible. No need to wait or ponder too much—just click, click, hooray! Our brains get that sweet dopamine hit almost immediately as we anticipate the arrival of our goodies. Retailers know this all too well, using algorithms that show us items we might like based on past buys or interests. They make the act of shopping feel personalised and urgent, which only fuels the fire of impulsivity.

Huge sales events, like the grand carnivals of commerce known as Black Friday or Cyber Monday, thrive on a concept called FOMO—the fear of missing out. Imagine this: everyone else is diving into deals, nabbing bargains left and right, and you do not want to be left behind, do you? This fear triggers our brain's amygdala, creating a sense of urgency. Marketers tap into this by highlighting limited time offers and exclusive discounts, pushing people to buy now and think later.

Fortunately, there are ways to combat the pull of impulse buying and regain control over our purchasing habits. One effective method is to develop mindful purchasing habits. Imagine becoming the zen master of shopping, where every buy is a thoughtful decision rather than a spur-of-the-moment craving. Here is how you can harness that inner wisdom:

- **Recognise Triggers:** Make note of when you feel the shopping itch. Is it after scrolling through social media, or maybe when you are bored out of your mind? Identifying these moments can help you steer clear of impulse buys.

- **Set Boundaries:** Establish rules, like a mandatory waiting period before big purchases. During this time, you will have the chance to evaluate whether the item aligns with your budget and needs.

- **Create Realistic Goals:** Define what you want from your shopping endeavours. Maybe it is sticking to essentials or saving up for something special rather than splurging on little distractions that add up.

By employing these strategies, you can start to rewire how your brain reacts to shopping stimuli. Instead of letting those dopamine bursts lead you astray, use them wisely to fuel positive choices. It is not about cutting out joy entirely—after all, shopping should be enjoyable—but about understanding the why behind each swipe of your credit card.

As you navigate the chaotic aisles of modern consumer culture, remember that knowledge is power. Understanding how stores and online platforms use dopamine as a tool to lure us into spending can arm you against the pitfalls of impulse buying.

Managing Digital Dopamine Triggers

Mindful media consumption is about awareness, being present, and distinguishing between necessary notifications and digital noise. Instead of mindlessly scrolling through feeds until your eyes glaze over, pause and ask yourself: "Is this adding value to my life?" If the answer leans toward "no," it might be time to shut down and look up—maybe even out of a window. Take breaks, slow down your online pace, and savour content like a fine vintage wine rather than chugging it like a can of pop. Your brain will thank you for the reduced overload.

This approach is not about completely cutting out digital media; rather, it is about being more intentional with your consumption. Think of it as savouring a delicious meal instead of wolfing down fast food. When you engage with content, try to be fully present. If you are watching a video, give it your full attention instead of letting it play in the background while you scroll through another app. This mindful approach can help you derive more value from the content you consume and reduce the feeling of being overwhelmed by information.

Next, let us gear up with technological assistance. Yes, the very thing causing the problem can help solve it, too! Enter technology management apps—your sidekicks in digital health. These apps monitor your screen time, provide insights into usage patterns, and set limits on app access. Treat them like that good friend who nudges you before you take the third slice of cake, offering gentle reminders to step away when you have been lost in a video rabbit hole for hours. The key is consistency and using data to encourage healthier habits. By knowing exactly how much time you spend online, you can make informed decisions about cutting down.

These apps can be eye-opening. You might be surprised to learn that you spend two hours a day on social media without even realising it. Armed with this knowledge, you can set realistic goals for reducing your screen time. Maybe start by aiming to cut 15 minutes off your daily social media use. These small changes can add up to significant improvements in your digital well-being over time.

Creating healthy digital environments is like feng shui for your tech space—it is all about balance and eliminating negative vibes. Start by considering your physical spaces at home: establishing tech-free zones can foster genuine interactions without the lure of notifications. Imagine a dining room table free from the pull of texts and email alerts, where conversations flow uninterrupted. Simultaneously, curate your online environment by unfollowing accounts that spark unnecessary envy or anxiety. Surround yourself with positive influences that uplift rather than drain. This proactive approach ensures a digital habitat conducive to your well-being, aligning more closely with your values and aspirations.

Think of your digital space as an extension of your physical space. Just as you would not fill your home with things that make you feel bad about yourself, do not fill your digital space with content that does the same. Be ruthless in curating your online experience. If a social media account consistently makes you feel inadequate or upset, it might be time to hit that unfollow button.

Change takes time, and there is no need to toss your phone into the ocean or retreat to a cabin in the woods (unless you want to). Starting small with manageable steps can lead to substantial improvements in your relationship with technology.

Remember, the goal is not to eliminate technology from your life but to create a healthier relationship with it. It is about finding a balance that works for you. Maybe you decide to have a "digital sunset" an hour before bed, turning off all screens to help your mind wind down. Or perhaps you choose one day a week to be a "low-tech day," where you minimise your screen time and focus on offline activities.

As you implement these strategies, pay attention to how you feel. You might notice improvements in your sleep, your ability to focus, or your overall mood. Celebrate these positive changes, no matter how small. Every step toward a healthier digital lifestyle is a step worth acknowledging.

Key Takeaways

- Dopamine interacts with our brains during activities related to technology, fast food, and shopping, driving our desire for instant gratification.

- Modern life often keeps dopamine levels elevated, making it easy to fall into patterns of impulsive consumption and constant engagement.

- The emphasis is on finding balance in our consumption habits, rather than seeking complete elimination of pleasurable activities.

- The goal is to discover healthier ways to enjoy life that do not rely on excessive digital or consumerist influences.

- Aim to reduce the impact of constant digital and consumerist stimuli on your mental and emotional well-being.

Chapter 5:

Dopamine and Decision-Making

Matt stared at his phone, his thumb hovering over the "Place Order" button. The late-night craving for pizza had struck again, and he found himself locked in an epic battle of willpower versus want.

"Come on, Matt, you promised yourself you would eat healthier," he muttered, even as his mouth watered at the thought of cheesy, doughy goodness.

Just then, his partner, Ash, wandered into the living room. "What is taking so long? You have been staring at that screen for ages."

Matt sighed dramatically. "I am trying to decide if I should order this pizza or be a responsible adult and eat the salad in the fridge."

Ash chuckled as he sat down on the sofa. "Ah, the age-old battle between dopamine and discipline. Let me guess, that pizza is winning right now?"

"Dopamine?" Matt raised an eyebrow. "Isn't that just the "feel-good" chemical?"

"Oh, mate," Ash grinned, leaning forward conspiratorially. "Dopamine is so much more than that. It is like the sneaky puppet master of our decisions. Right now, it is probably doing a happy dance in your brain at the mere thought of that pizza."

Matt looked at his phone, then back at Ash, intrigued. "You mean this little molecule is behind my inability to resist late-night snacks?"

"That is just the tip of the iceberg," Ash replied, his eyes twinkling with amusement. "Get ready! You are about to learn why that pizza seems more appealing than world peace right now. Trust me, it is going to change the way you look at every decision you make."

As Ash launched into his explanation, Matt settled in, his pizza craving momentarily forgotten. Little did he know, he was about to embark on a journey of self-discovery that would leave him seeing his daily choices in a whole new light.

Decision Fatigue and Dopamine

Imagine you have been staring at your screen for what feels like forever, trying to choose between Chinese takeaway or pizza for dinner. The decision seems monumental, yet you cannot seem to make it. This is decision fatigue—a sneaky little gremlin that creeps in when you have been making too many choices in a row. It is not just about food, though; it impacts all kinds of decisions we face daily. At its core, it is the brain's tiredness after a long session of choosing, leading to poorer judgment.

Now, let us dive deeper into what is happening inside your brain when you hit this fatigue. Our trusty neurotransmitter, dopamine, plays a crucial role here. Often dubbed the "feel-good" chemical, dopamine is not just about chasing rewards; it is also about evaluating potential outcomes and guiding us through decisions. However, every choice drains a little bit of that treasured dopamine reservoir. Over time, especially on days filled with non-stop decision-making, our dopamine levels can dip significantly. Recognising this depletion helps us understand why, after a slew of decisions, we tend to go for the convenient option.

Think of it like your phone battery. You start strong in the morning, but by dinner time, you are down to 5% and frantically searching for a charger. The brain's dopamine functions similarly—each choice chips away at those levels, leaving you weary and more prone to taking shortcuts. This might lead to decisions like purchasing an expensive item without much thought during a late-night shopping spree or opting for junk food simply because it is there.

There are ways to combat decision fatigue. One effective strategy is to recognise that managing your choices consciously can boost the quality of your decisions. Let us say you tend to scroll through endless film options on streaming services. By setting pre-decided criteria—such as choosing based on genre, director, or any other factor—you streamline the process, conserving that precious dopamine. Managing decisions does not mean eliminating choices entirely; rather, it involves wisely prioritising them. In this way, you save energy for when it really counts, like deciding whether to accept that job offer or move to another city.

Ignoring decision fatigue can lead to poor choices. Ever noticed how late-night snack choices tend to be less than ideal? It is not just the allure of the midnight toastie; it is also the result of your brain taking a break from non-stop decision-making throughout the day. When faced with tired neurons and dwindling dopamine, we are more likely to grab the easiest thing rather than what is best.

Consider the likes of Steve Jobs and Elon Musk, who swear by wearing the same thing every day. It is not just about looking chic; they are also protecting themselves against decision fatigue. By minimising daily choices, they reserve their mental energy for more pressing decisions. That is a wise approach, as it ensures they remain mentally sharp for the choices that truly matter.

You can combat decision fatigue by understanding your limits. Much like a marathon runner who knows their pace, recognise when your brain needs a break. Short respites, even if just for a moment, can rejuvenate those depleted dopamine levels.

Ultimately, it is about being aware of the sneaky effects of decision fatigue and how dopamine influences our choices. With this knowledge, we can better navigate our day-to-day lives, sidestepping the traps of hastily made decisions.

Risk-Taking Behaviours

Dopamine, the brain's "feel-good" chemical, plays a starring role in our willingness to take risks. It is like that friend who always suggests turning left instead of right, often leading you on unexpected—and occasionally precarious—adventures.

Interestingly, studies have shown that higher levels of dopamine are linked to increased risk-taking behaviours. In experiments conducted with Long-Evans rats, scientists discovered that dopamine release in specific brain regions significantly influenced the tendency to make risky choices (Freels et al., 2020). This correlation does not just exist in rodent brains; it mirrors human behaviour as well. Whether it is deciding to invest in volatile stocks or opting for an impromptu skydive without considering fear of heights, elevated dopamine levels can nudge people toward risky decisions.

Our internal assessment of risk can become skewed under the influence of dopamine. Imagine driving through a dense cloud of mist; your usual landmarks look distorted, making navigation tricky. Similarly, when dopamine floods the brain, it clouds judgement, potentially altering life trajectories. People might find themselves zigzagging through career choices or relationship decisions based on momentary thrills rather than long-term goals. Such clouded assessments can sometimes lead to impulsive decisions with unforeseen consequences—a reality not just limited to gaming tables in Vegas but extending into everyday life choices.

Real-life instances of heightened dopamine effects are not hard to find. Picture someone staggering out of a meeting where they have been praised to high heaven, feeling invincible. This dopamine-fuelled high might lead them to celebrate with an extravagant purchase they have not budgeted for, leaving them scratching their heads at the end of the month. Dopamine can turn us into impulse buyers, adrenaline junkies, or unwitting gamblers in the grand casino of life.

If you are prone to these whims, embracing mindfulness can help balance the scales of risk-reward analysis. It is akin to hitting pause during a heated moment, allowing yourself a chance to breathe and evaluate. By slowing down and paying attention to the present moment, you can gain clarity over emotional surges driven by dopamine. Mindfulness encourages people to ask critical questions: What is the genuine reward here? Is the risk worth the thrill? These moments of reflection can anchor decision-makers, steering them toward choices that align better with their values and long-term intentions.

Consider John, who stands at a crossroads about whether to invest his savings in a flashy tech startup promising astronomical returns. With dopamine whispering sweet nothings of potential wealth in his ear, mindfulness could bring him back to basics. He might weigh the decision against his personal financial goals, family commitments, and the real-world volatility of startups. Instead of diving headfirst into uncharted waters, he practises patience and informed deliberation, helping him make a wiser decision.

Cognitive Biases Linked to Dopamine

Imagine you are standing in front of an ice cream van. Your brain, flooded with dopamine from past joyful experiences with ice cream, whispers sweet nothings about how today's Mr. Whippy will be the best you have ever tasted. This is optimism bias in action, making you overestimate the positive outcome of your decision. Influenced by dopamine, optimism bias leads us to expect favourable outcomes, even when they are unlikely. It is why some of us still believe that buying a lottery ticket might mean retiring on a tropical island soon. While it is lovely to remain optimistic, this bias can often blindside us from recognising realistic risks or negative possibilities, leaving us less prepared for setbacks.

Let us talk about the recency effect. You may have noticed that recent experiences, especially if they are filled with dopamine, dominate your decisions. That is the recency effect charming your brain. If last week's dinner at a new restaurant was delightful, thanks to all those dopamine rewards, you might decide to go there again tonight, overlooking other potentially great venues. Our inclination to give more weight to the latest information makes it tough to stay objective.

Understanding these biases does not mean we are doomed to be controlled by them. Luckily, the art of slow thinking offers a pathway to navigate through these biases. Slow thinking means you take a leisurely stroll down Decision Street rather than racing through it. When we slow down, we provide ourselves with the grace period to weigh all our options, evaluate evidence, and confront biases head-on. It is like pressing pause to listen to the whole story before jumping to a conclusion. By consciously engaging in this deliberate process, we can substantially improve our decision quality.

One practical strategy is to start by acknowledging that our dopamine-driven brains are not always our best decision-makers, especially when the stakes are high. Each time you find yourself overly optimistic or stuck in a loop of recent memories while making a decision, mentally step back. Ask yourself, "Is my brain being honest here, or is it just riding a wave of dopamine?" Just posing this question can disrupt automatic, biased thinking patterns.

To further combat these biases, consider keeping a decision-making journal. Writing down the choices you made, the context and the emotions involved provides a clearer picture over time. This practice can help you identify patterns where dopamine may have led you astray with biases like optimism or the recency effect.

Let us also remember group dynamics. Just as one overly enthusiastic friend can influence the group's plans, heightened dopamine levels can lead to collective optimism among teams, causing them to overlook challenges. Encourage discussions that invite scepticism and critical thinking, thereby allowing diverse perspectives to shine through.

Ultimately, understanding and managing these dopamine-influenced biases is not about erasing them. That would be like trying to silence your inner cheerleader permanently. Instead, it is about cultivating awareness so that we can make informed, balanced, and well-considered decisions despite their presence. After all, the goal is not to live a life devoid of joy-inducing dopamine moments; it is to enjoy them while ensuring they do not hijack our capacity for sound judgment.

Strategies to Improve Decision-Making Skills

To navigate this dopamine-driven maze effectively, practical strategies can help enhance our decision-making abilities and empower us to make more deliberate choices with less stress.

First up on our list of strategies is mindfulness. Picture your mind as a crowded attic; practising mindfulness is akin to decluttering it. It helps you become more aware of your thoughts and emotions without judgment, offering clarity and stability. This calming practice reduces impulsivity, allowing you to process decisions with a clear head rather than racing along dopamine-fuelled whims. According to Kirk et al. (2016), mindfulness training has been shown to increase cooperative behaviour and emotional regulation, which are beneficial for more thoughtful decision-making.

Now, let us dive into some frameworks that act like a GPS for decision-making—decision matrices! Imagine standing at a crossroads with multiple potential paths. Decision matrices lay out options systematically, factoring in various attributes like importance, cost, or time. This method encourages systematic thinking, making it harder for those pesky dopamine impulses to lead you astray.

Another profound tool in our decision-making arsenal is aligning choices with personal values. Let's face it—dopamine loves shiny new things and sugar rushes, often pulling us toward short-term pleasures. When you tether your decisions to your core values, you create a sturdy anchor against these temptations. Whether it is health, honesty, or personal growth, identifying what truly matters to you acts as a compass, guiding your choices and ensuring they resonate with your authentic self.

Here is a curveball—ever considered reversing your decisions? This technique involves revisiting previous choices and analysing what would have happened if you had made the opposite call. Decision reversal can be illuminating. You may uncover patterns in your decision-making habits or discover areas where dopamine's influence was less than stellar. This exercise not only enhances self-awareness but also provides insights for improving future decisions.

Balancing variety and simplicity in decision-making is another critical aspect. While a multitude of options might seem appealing, it can overwhelm your brain's decision-making capacity, leading to analysis paralysis. Imagine you are at a buffet with endless choices; instead of feeling delighted, you might feel indecisive. Devising systems that offer just enough variety without flooding your mental circuits is vital. Streamlining decisions to essential elements preserves your dopamine reserves and leads to greater satisfaction.

Key Takeaways

- Dopamine plays a crucial role in our decision-making process, influencing a wide range of choices from mundane (such as food selection) to significant (like engaging in risky activities).

- Decision fatigue is a real phenomenon that can impair our ability to make sound choices over time.

- Various tools and techniques are available to help manage impulsive decisions driven by dopamine surges.

- Practising mindfulness is a valuable strategy for fostering more conscious and deliberate decision-making.

- Understanding dopamine's influence can aid in avoiding impulse purchases and unhealthy choices.

- Striking a balance between caution and the feel-good effects of dopamine is essential for making wise decisions.

Chapter 6:

Habits: The Good, the Bad, and the Dopamine

It is 3 p.m. on a typical workday. Mei, a marketing executive, finds herself reaching for her phone without even realising it. Her fingers move automatically, opening the social media app she has been trying to cut back on. Before she knows it, fifteen minutes have vanished, and she is still scrolling through an endless feed of photos and status updates.

"How did I end up here again?" she wonders, a mix of frustration and curiosity washing over her.

Mei's experience is far from unique; it is a perfect example of how habits, fuelled by the brain's reward system, can take control of our actions almost invisibly.

As Mei puts her phone down, determined to focus on her work, she cannot help but ponder the force behind this automatic behaviour. Little does she know that a tiny molecule called dopamine is playing a significant role in this daily dance of distraction.

In this chapter, we will unravel the mystery behind Mei's seemingly involuntary phone check and countless other habits that shape our lives. We will explore how dopamine, that sneaky little neurotransmitter, acts as the behind-the-scenes director of our routines, making some behaviours irresistibly appealing while others feel like a drain.

From the moment Mei's hand first moved toward her phone to the satisfaction she felt while scrolling, dopamine was there, orchestrating every step. By understanding this intricate relationship between our brain chemistry and our actions, we can gain insight into why breaking bad habits feels like an uphill battle and why forming new, beneficial ones can be so rewarding.

So, let us dive into the fascinating world of dopamine and habit formation. Who knows? By the end of this chapter, you might just look at your own quirky routines with fresh eyes and a newfound appreciation for the complex biological processes at play.

How Habits Are Formed in the Brain

Dopamine plays an important role in forming habits in the brain. At the core of habit formation is something known as the "habit loop." Imagine this loop as your brain's very own cycle track, featuring three main stages: cue, routine, and reward. Each stage acts like a pit stop, guiding you through your daily behaviours. The cue is a trigger—perhaps the smell of fresh coffee that nudges you toward brewing a cup. The routine is the action itself—making that delightful drink. The reward is the satisfaction or boost you feel after enjoying it. This cycle helps us identify what sparks certain behaviours and how they become part of our daily fabric.

When we engage in habitual actions, the release of dopamine signals pleasure, acting like a stamp of approval from your internal cheerleader. That is why drinking coffee is so strongly linked with a happy feeling. This chemical reinforcement ensures you remember just how enjoyable that action was, paving the way for its repetition in the future. So each time you get your coffee fix and dopamine kicks in, it is like your brain saying, "Well done! Let us do it again soon."

The brain also possesses an amazing ability to transform itself—neuroplasticity. It is like having an artist in your brain, constantly reshaping and repainting your neural pathways based on the experiences and habits you engage in. Think of this plasticity as your brain's personal trainer, always ready to teach those neurons new tricks or rewrite old scripts. This flexibility allows us to establish new habits and tweak existing ones. Whether you are learning to hit the gym regularly or trying to cut down on junk food, neuroplasticity is there, moulding your brain to support these changes.

Our environment has a sneaky way of influencing how habits take hold and stick. Ever notice how walking into a cinema makes you crave popcorn, even if you just had lunch? That is the power of environmental cues. Our surroundings provide constant nudges and reminders that can either reinforce or challenge our habits. Picture yourself stepping into a library—suddenly, you might find yourself whispering instead of speaking loudly. It is these contextual hints that keep habits ticking, adding layers of subtlety to our behaviour.

Understanding the habit loop comes with practical benefits, too. By recognising these cues and rewards, we can consciously design our environments and routines to foster positive habits while minimising the not-so-healthy ones. If the morning sunlight triggers you to grab your phone first thing, consider placing it a little further out of reach or replacing that habit with a few minutes of stretching or meditation. Leveraging this understanding empowers us to break free from automatic behaviours and create a life that is more aligned with our long-term goals and values.

Dopamine is also deeply intertwined with motivation and perseverance. This neurotransmitter acts like an energetic motivational speaker in your head, keeping you returning to those rewarding actions. It drives the persistence needed to build and maintain habits. So when you are trying to stick with a new fitness routine or learn a musical instrument, dopamine's encouragement helps push you past the initial hurdles.

And let us not forget the adaptable nature of our brains. Neuroplasticity offers hope and encouragement for anyone looking to make lasting changes. While it may seem daunting to change a deeply ingrained habit, knowing that your brain is equipped to rewire itself can be incredibly empowering. It is like having an eraser next to a chalkboard, allowing you to adjust your behavioural patterns and draw new pathways over time.

The influence of our environment is another key player in the habit game. The spaces where we live, work, and socialise have hidden levers that can either sabotage or support our efforts to change. For instance, if you are trying to eat healthier, the layout of your kitchen or your grocery shopping habits could inadvertently prompt better nutritional choices. Being aware of these external factors lets you tweak your surroundings—keeping healthy snacks visible and less nutritious options out of sight.

As we continue to explore how habits are formed and maintained, it is clear that they are not just simple routines we pick up by chance. Instead, they result from a complex interplay of neurological processes, chemical reinforcements, and environmental influences.

Breaking Bad Habits and Forming Good Ones

Let us talk about identifying habits that are not doing us any favours. Maybe it is stress that sends you running to the fridge or boredom that has you scrolling endlessly. Once you pinpoint what triggers these behaviours, you have taken a giant leap toward changing them.

Consider Sally, who reached for her phone every time she felt a twinge of anxiety. It was almost automatic—when a notification pinged, her hand would dart out before she even realised it. By keeping a simple journal for a week, Sally noticed this pattern and began addressing the root cause of her anxiety instead of just distracting herself with social media.

Or think about Mike, who could not resist the office vending machine every afternoon around 3 p.m. After some reflection, he realised it was not hunger driving him to snack, but a combination of boredom and a need for a quick energy boost. This awareness allowed him to plan more engaging tasks for that time of day and pack healthier, energy-sustaining snacks.

Now, let us move on to the "10% Rule." No, it is not a sales discount. It is about making changes gradually so they stick. Imagine trying to wake up at 5 a.m. after years of sleeping in until midday. Start by waking up 10% earlier each week until you reach your goal. The same applies to cutting back on digital distractions: reduce your screen time by 10%, and soon enough, you will be able to endure a dinner without checking notifications. This approach might sound like slowly pulling off a plaster, but trust me, it is less painful and more effective.

Take Lisa, for example. She wanted to cut down on her daily four cups of coffee but found the idea of going cold turkey terrifying. Instead, she began reducing her intake by just half a cup per week. Six weeks later, she was down to two cups a day and feeling great—without the headaches and irritability that often accompany sudden caffeine withdrawal.

Then there is the replacement strategy. This involves swapping out bad habits for better ones, much like exchanging an old, worn-out sweater for a new, cosy one. Instead of reaching for that mid-afternoon biscuit, take a short walk. Swap your Netflix binge for a good book. These small substitutions help rewire your brain to crave healthier, more fulfilling activities. Just remember, it is a marathon, and change does not happen overnight.

John, a self-proclaimed couch potato, decided to replace one episode of his nightly TV show with a 20-minute yoga session. At first, it felt weird and uncomfortable. But after a few weeks, he began looking forward to that peaceful time on the mat. He did not give up TV entirely, but he created a healthier balance in his routine.

What about the dopamine connection? Our brains love a good dose of dopamine—it is like our internal high-five machine. Every time you indulge a habit, your brain lights up with dopamine, rewarding you like a puppy when you scratch its ears. When you introduce new, healthier habits, your brain starts associating these replacements with rewards too. The goal is to gently guide your brain away from destructive patterns toward something better—like substituting your guilty pleasure midnight snack with a fun dance session in your kitchen.

Remember Emma, who used to end every night with a bowl of ice cream? She started playing her favourite upbeat songs and having a mini dance party instead. At first, it felt silly and not nearly as satisfying as the ice cream. But over time, her brain began to associate this fun, energetic activity with an end-of-day reward. Now, she looks forward to her dance sessions and feels much better afterwards than she did after her ice cream binges.

All this might sound like TED Talk material, but remember, it is all about embracing change, experimenting with new strategies, and adjusting along the way. If you stumble, do not worry; we all do. There is nothing wrong with starting again. The art of habit-changing is a blend of creativity, resilience, and possibly a pinch of humour. After all, would we have made it through childhood piano lessons without giggling over some off-key notes? I think not.

Take Alex, who decided to start a meditation practice. His first attempt was a disaster—he fell asleep and woke up an hour later, late for work. The second time, he could not stop thinking about his to-do list. By the fifth try, he was still struggling to focus, but he could laugh at his wandering thoughts instead of getting frustrated. Now, six months in, he is not a Zen master, but he has found a routine that works for him and helps him start the day on a calmer note.

So go ahead. Turn off your phone with pride, swap that chocolate bar for a fruit slice, and unplug from the digital noise for a few hours. Dopamine and your well-being will thank you later—with a genuine internal applause that feels even better than scoring extra likes on a random post.

Remember, the goal is not perfection—it is progress. You might not transform into a morning person overnight, but you may find yourself enjoying the quiet of early mornings a few days a week. Perhaps you will not completely kick your social media habit, but you might rediscover the joy of reading a physical book before bed.

Let us not forget the power of celebrating small wins. Did you choose a piece of fruit over a biscuit today? That is worth a mental high-five. Did you resist the urge to check your phone during dinner? Pat yourself on the back. These small victories add up over time, reinforcing your new habits and boosting your confidence in your ability to change.

Remember, changing habits is a personal journey. What works for your friend might not work for you, and that is okay. Maybe you find you need accountability, so you join a support group or team up with a friend who is also trying to make changes. Or perhaps you discover that you are motivated by tracking your progress, so you start using a habit-tracking app or a good old-fashioned sticker chart (who says those are just for children?).

The key is to stay curious and keep experimenting. Treat this process like a scientific experiment, with you as both the scientist and the subject. What happens if you try meditating in the morning instead of at night? How do you feel when you swap your usual sugary breakfast for a protein-packed option? By approaching habit change with this mindset, you turn what could be a frustrating process into an interesting journey of self-discovery.

As you embark on your habit-changing adventure, remember to be patient with yourself, celebrate the small wins, and do not be afraid to laugh at the inevitable hiccups along the way. Your brain's reward system will gradually adjust, and before you know it, you might find yourself craving that morning jog or looking forward to your veg-packed lunch. Here's to healthier habits and a happier, more balanced you!

Role of Reinforcement in Habit Loops

Reinforcement plays a starring role in shaping our daily routines. Every habit we form is like a little drama inside our brains, and reinforcement is the director calling the shots.

Positive reinforcement is the star of this show. Imagine you are training a dog to sit. Each time it does, you give it a treat, and soon enough, it is sitting on command like a pro. In human terms, positive reinforcement is when we reward ourselves for doing something good, making it more likely we will do it again. It is the dopamine release—the brain's happy dance—that hooks us. Whether it is a sense of accomplishment after finishing a task or treating yourself to a delicious snack, positive reinforcement strengthens the neural pathways that keep these behaviours coming back.

Negative reinforcement, on the other hand, is not punishment; it is more like a type of avoidance game. Let us say you do not like getting caught in traffic (who does?). You discover that leaving home 10 minutes earlier avoids the jam. In this case, you have just reinforced an early departure habit by avoiding a negative experience.

So, how do we leverage these reinforcement techniques to shape our daily lives? Simple steps make all the difference. Start by setting clear goals. Whether it is exercising regularly or cutting back on screen time, knowing what you want is key. Celebrate those small wins with rewards that matter to you. Did you hit the gym five days in a row? Great! Binge your favourite show guilt-free! This mix of goal setting and enjoyment keeps motivation levels high and habits sticking around.

This is where habit stacking comes into play. It is like building with LEGO bricks—stacking new habits on top of existing ones to reinforce them. Let us break it down:

1. **Identify Current Habits:** Think about your day-to-day rituals—like your morning coffee or evening walk. These are golden opportunities for habit stacking.

2. **Choose a New Habit:** Want to meditate more? Read every day? Pick something manageable and straightforward to begin with.

3. **Stack the Habits:** Attach this new habit to an old one. For example, meditate right after your morning brew or read during lunch. It is all about pairing routines for smooth sailing.

4. **Consistency is Key:** Stick to your new combined routine to strengthen those brain connections. Remember, Rome was not built in a day, and neither are habits!

5. **Ramp Up the Rewards:** Ensure the outcomes are worthwhile—whether it is feeling zen post-meditation or becoming a knowledge maven through reading.

6. **Celebrate Success:** High-five yourself for each milestone. Acknowledge your progress, however small, reinforcing the loop of positivity and motivation.

Case Study of Successful Habit Change

Meet Javier, a 32-year-old software developer who struggled to maintain a healthy work-life balance. He often found himself working late into the night, skipping meals, and neglecting his physical health. It was when he realised that his habits were affecting both his job performance and personal relationships that he decided it was time for a change. Javier's goal was to establish a healthier routine that would improve his productivity at work and allow for more personal time.

Javier faced several initial challenges: he had difficulty setting boundaries between work and personal life, suffered from a poor sleep schedule due to late-night work sessions, had irregular eating habits, lacked exercise, and constantly felt overwhelmed and stressed.

To address these issues, Javier developed an action plan. He decided to set a strict work schedule, implement a wind-down routine to improve his sleep, start meal planning and prep, integrate daily exercise, and practice mindfulness through meditation.

The implementation of Javier's plan was not without struggles. In the first two weeks, he often worked past his set end time and found meal prepping time-consuming, but he persevered. By weeks three and four, he began to see the benefits of his new routine. His energy levels increased, and he became more focused during work hours. Between weeks five and eight, Javier consistently ended work on time and enjoyed his evening activities.

His colleagues even noticed his improved mood and efficiency. After six months, Javier had successfully transformed his daily routine: his work productivity increased by 20%, his sleep quality improved significantly, he lost half a stone, his stress levels decreased, and he experienced improved relationships with friends and family due to more available personal time. The new habits had become second nature, and Javier even found time to start a new hobby—painting.

Javier's case demonstrates several key takeaways about successful habit change. Consistency was crucial; his commitment to sticking with his new routines, even when they were difficult, was key to his success. He also learned that small changes add up—each change seemed minor, but together they created a significant lifestyle shift.

Patience played a vital role, as it took several weeks before Javier saw noticeable benefits. His holistic approach, addressing multiple areas of his life simultaneously, led to comprehensive improvements in his overall well-being. Finally, Javier experienced positive ripple effects, as improving his habits had unexpected positive impacts on his professional life and relationships.

Javier's success stemmed from setting clear goals, creating a structured plan, and committing to gradual, sustainable changes. His story serves as an inspiring example of how anyone can transform their life through dedicated habit change.

Key Takeaways

- The brain's habit-forming mechanisms, including the habit loop and the role of dopamine, are complex yet understandable processes that influence our daily behaviours and routines.

- Understanding these neurological processes empowers us to actively shape our habits instead of being passive participants in their formation and maintenance.

- Successful habit change involves recognising cues, adjusting routines, celebrating small wins, and leveraging the brain's reward system to reinforce positive behaviours over time.

Chapter 7:

Practical Techniques for Better Choices

Zara stood in line at her favourite local coffee shop, tapping her foot to the rhythm of the espresso machines whirring in the background. The warm, inviting aroma of freshly ground coffee beans wafted through the air, but it was the display case of sweet things that caught her eye as she inched closer to the counter.

There it was—a decadent chocolate chip cookie, still slightly warm from the oven, its edges perfectly crisp and centre promising to be delightfully gooey. Zara's mouth watered as she remembered the last time she had indulged in one of these heavenly creations. "Just a latte today," she muttered to herself, trying to summon her willpower. But as she approached the counter, that little voice in her head grew louder. "You have had a tough week," it whispered. "You deserve a treat."

Zara hesitated, her internal struggle playing out as clearly as day on her face. Milo, the barista who knew her usual order by heart, raised an eyebrow. "The usual... plus a cookie today?" he asked with a knowing smile. At that moment, Zara felt like a character in a cartoon, with an angel on one shoulder and a devil on the other. The angel reminded her of the gym membership she had just renewed and the healthy eating plan she had been following. The devil, on the other hand, painted a vivid picture of the blissful moment that cookie would touch her lips.

Little did Zara know, the real puppeteer behind this mental tug-of-war was a neurotransmitter called dopamine, flooding her brain's reward centres and making that cookie seem like the most important decision of her life.

As she opened her mouth to respond to Milo, Zara's phone buzzed. It was a message from her friend Aisha: "Great job sticking to your goals this week! Can't wait for our hike tomorrow!"

Zara smiled, feeling a different kind of warmth spread through her chest.

"Just the latte today, Milo," she said, surprising even herself with the decisiveness in her voice.

As Zara waited for her drink, she realised that the satisfaction of staying true to her goals felt even better than the momentary pleasure that cookie would have brought. She made a mental note to look up why seemingly simple decisions could feel so complicated sometimes.

Delaying Gratification Effectively

Let us take a look at delayed gratification and how it can lead to better life outcomes. Picture this: you are hungry, and there is a delicious treat right in front of you—a delectable marshmallow staring back with sugary temptation. The Marshmallow Experiment offers a glimpse into self-control. The children who resisted the urge to devour that single marshmallow immediately in anticipation of getting two later often scored significant brownie points later in life—academically, socially, and even professionally. Patience really pays off.

This famous experiment, conducted by psychologist Walter Mischel in the 1960s, has become a cornerstone in understanding the power of delayed gratification. The children who managed to wait for the second marshmallow demonstrated not just willpower but also the ability to create strategies to distract themselves from temptation. Some sang songs, while others covered their eyes or pretended the marshmallow was something less appealing. These early signs of self-regulation turned out to be predictive of future success.

So, why does waiting for that second marshmallow matter so much? It is about building self-control muscles, which are pivotal in navigating life's challenges and opportunities. Those who master this skill tend to fare better because they learn to manage impulses effectively, setting themselves up for long-term satisfaction rather than instant gratification.

Think about your own life. How often have you made a snap decision you later regretted? Perhaps it was an impulse purchase that left your wallet lighter and your wardrobe full of things you did not really need. Or maybe it was choosing the comfort of the sofa over a workout, leaving you feeling guilty and less healthy in the long run. The ability to delay gratification allows us to make decisions that align with our long-term goals and values, rather than being swayed by momentary desires.

Now, let us switch gears and talk about how you can harness the power of delaying immediate rewards in your daily life. Say you are browsing online, and that flashy new gadget catches your eye. Before hitting that "Buy Now" button, try the 10-minute rule. Here is how it works: take a breather, let ten minutes pass, and use this time to weigh the necessity against the alluring impulse. Often, you will find that the urge subsides, and you no longer feel an urgent need to buy the product. This technique acts as your mental filter, helping you distinguish needs from wants. Just this little pause can help you avoid regretful splurges.

This 10-minute rule can be applied to various aspects of life. Feeling the urge to check your phone during work? Wait 10 minutes. Tempted to snack even though you are not really hungry? Give it 10 minutes. This small delay allows your rational mind to catch up with your impulsive desires, often leading to better decisions.

Visualise this next scenario: you have big goals—career, personal, financial. Yet the struggle to keep your eyes on these future prizes often gets disrupted by immediate distractions. By picturing yourself achieving these goals and savouring those positive consequences, you reinforce discipline and focus. Imagine the pride and sense of achievement when you hit that milestone. Visualisation is not just thinking; it is training your brain to stay aligned with long-term aspirations, making them tangible targets rather than fleeting daydreams.

For instance, if your goal is to save for a down payment on a house, do not just think about the number in your bank account. Visualise yourself walking through the front door of your new home, arranging furniture in your living room, or hosting friends for a housewarming party. This vivid mental imagery can make the abstract concept of saving money feel more real and immediate, helping you resist the temptation to spend on less important things.

Let us talk about accountability partners—those unsung heroes in your journey toward self-discipline. Bringing someone else into your goals creates a social commitment, a shared voyage where you both promise to steer clear of short-lived temptations. When you are about to falter, your accountability partner can pull you back on course, reminding you of the bigger prize. It nurtures collective discipline, making the challenge seem less daunting. After all, camaraderie can be an incredible motivator, adding layers of encouragement to delay gratification.

Your accountability partner does not have to share the same goals as you. The key is finding someone who understands the importance of what you are trying to achieve and is willing to support you. This could be a friend, family member, or even a professional coach. Regular check-ins with your accountability partner can help you stay on track and provide a space to celebrate small victories along the way.

As adults, whether we are overwhelmed by life's buffet of unhealthy choices or simply trying to navigate decision-making without slipping, we need strategies that stick. Delaying gratification stands out as an invaluable strategy, promising long-lasting satisfaction over transient thrills.

However, it is important to remember that delaying gratification does not mean never enjoying life's pleasures. The key is balance and mindful decision-making. Sometimes, it is okay to indulge in that piece of cake or buy that concert ticket. The goal is to make these choices consciously rather than impulsively, ensuring they align with your overall well-being and goals.

Practising delayed gratification can also positively impact your mental health. It can reduce stress and anxiety associated with impulsive decisions and their consequences. Moreover, the sense of accomplishment that comes from achieving long-term goals can boost self-esteem and overall life satisfaction.

In our increasingly fast-paced, instant-gratification-oriented world, the ability to delay gratification is more valuable than ever. It is a skill that can be developed and strengthened over time, much like a muscle. Start small—maybe with that 10-

minute rule—and gradually work your way up to bigger challenges.

Remember, the path to success and fulfilment is not always about grand gestures or dramatic changes. Often, it is about the small, consistent choices we make day after day. By cultivating the ability to delay gratification, we are essentially investing in our future selves, creating a foundation for success and satisfaction that goes far beyond the fleeting pleasure of instant rewards.

So, the next time you are faced with a "marshmallow moment," take a pause. Consider the bigger picture. Your future self will thank you for the wisdom and restraint you show today. After all, good things really do come to those who wait—especially when that wait is strategic, purposeful, and aligned with your long-term goals.

Creating a Rewarding Environment

Your environment has more impact on your decision-making than you might think. From the arrangement of furniture to the snacks lurking in your kitchen cabinets, these seemingly trivial elements can either steer you toward better choices or trip you up like a banana peel in a cartoon.

Designing Your Physical Space

Let us start with your physical space. Imagine walking into your kitchen and finding a bowl of vibrant fruits on the counter instead of a box of doughnuts taking centre stage. This is not just about aesthetics; it is about psychology! By strategically placing healthier options in plain sight, you are nudging yourself—and anyone else who wanders through—to choose a juicy apple over a sugary snack. You can make good habits easier by reducing friction between yourself and wise choices.

On the flip side, banish distractions from your workspace. Who can focus with a mini carnival of notifications buzzing and jingling at them like an overexcited electronic puppy?

Positive Reinforcement

Now, let us dive into the land of positive reinforcement, where rewards and behaviour meet in a motivational tango. For instance, after completing a challenging task, treat yourself to a mini chocolate bar or take a quick dance break to your favourite tune. Associating achievements with small rewards tricks your brain into linking hard work with a dopamine rush. This creates a feedback loop where effort equals fun, encouraging you to re-engage with tasks you might otherwise loathe. It is like training a puppy—but for humans. Try it out: complete a task and reward yourself a little. It is surprisingly effective!

Harnessing Technology

Technology can be both a massive procrastination magnet and a powerful tool when used wisely. Download apps that help track goals, send timely reminders, or record progress. Instead of getting sucked into endless doom-scrolling, transform your device into a digital coach that pulls you back when you veer off track. Think of it as wearing a fitness tracker for your life—it keeps you accountable, enhancing your journey toward better choices. Setting digital boundaries is like being that strict but loving parent who insists on curfews and vegetables.

Surrounding Yourself with Positivity

Have you ever noticed that hanging out with optimistic people lifts your spirits, while negativity spreads faster than bad gossip? Surrounding yourself with supportive friends or coworkers acts like a social safety net, cushioning you from slipping back into poor habits. When you associate with those who encourage wise decisions and aim high, you are likely to absorb some of that positive energy. Seek relationships that contribute positively to your well-being and watch how effortlessly your choices begin levelling up.

Visualising Success

Picture yourself as the poster child for healthy choices: you are in your meticulously organised, distraction-free office, munching on almonds next to your laptop. Your phone buzzes with a notification from the goal-tracking app you installed, reminding you to stand up and stretch after hours of focus. You decide to reward yourself with a tiny square of chocolate for completing another successful task. Meanwhile, your friend texts, cheering on your progress. Now, that is the way to get things done!

Mindfulness and Self-Awareness Practices

Mindfulness can significantly improve your decision-making by keeping those sneaky impulses in check. Contrary to popular belief, mindfulness is not just about sitting cross-legged on a mountaintop; it is a practical technique you can incorporate into your daily life to navigate the chaotic world of decision-making.

The Power of Meditation

Picture this: you are settled on a yoga mat with your eyes closed, breathing in tranquillity and exhaling stress like a pro. Meditation is not solely about tuning out; it is about tuning in. This practice heightens your awareness of thoughts and emotions, which is crucial for curbing knee-jerk reactions. Imagine facing an emotional trigger—whether it is someone eating the last slice of pizza or a sudden urge to splurge on yet another pair of shoes online. Regular meditation helps create a pause button between thought and action, enabling you to respond thoughtfully rather than impulsively.

Daily Journaling as Reflection

Let us talk about daily journaling. This practice serves as a reflective mirror for your mind, allowing you to document your thoughts surrounding choices. By jotting down your experiences and feelings, you gain insights into the triggers behind certain decisions. For instance, if you notice that every time you have a stressful day at work, you end up devouring an entire pint of tub cream, that is a clear trigger! Recognising these patterns allows you to strategise and mitigate impulses before they take over. It is like being your own detective, piecing together clues about your behaviour.

Identifying Triggers

Identifying triggers deserves some spotlight. It is akin to confronting the archenemies of your self-control head-on. Understanding what sets off an unhealthy dopamine response is key to managing it. By pinpointing the sources of your urges—whether it is late-night scrolling through social media or notifications from your favourite shopping app—you can arm yourself with preventative measures to combat these impulses.

Controlled Breathing Techniques

Sometimes all you need is a breather—quite literally. Controlled breathing is not just some zen-like exercise to practise in a lotus pose; it is a versatile tool you can use anywhere—when stuck in traffic, waiting for the kettle to boil, or before hitting "send" on that risky email. Breathing exercises teach you to regulate your emotional responses. When faced with an impulse, taking deep breaths can stabilise your racing heart and frantic mind, creating space for evaluation and deliberate action instead of impulsive reactions. This simple act can transform a moment of potential chaos into calm clarity.

Building Awareness Over Time

Incorporating these mindfulness practices does not mean instant transformation; it is about building awareness over time. Think of them as mental workouts—not for six-pack abs, but for a clear, focused mind. While you may not instantly become an unflappable Zen master, each practice chips away at impulsivity's control, bringing you closer to making healthier choices aligned with your long-term goals.

Building Stronger Willpower

Strengthening your willpower is akin to training for a mental marathon. Just as you would not start by running 26 miles right out of the gate, you should begin with smaller challenges, gradually building your stamina and resilience over time. This gradual exposure to tempting situations can be surprisingly effective. It is about controlling these exposures just enough to let your resistance flex its muscles.

For instance, if you are trying to resist the allure of sweets, start by allowing yourself a manageable indulgence level that challenges you without overwhelming you. Over time, you can increase your resilience by incrementally reducing your intake or only indulging at specific times, enhancing your ability to withstand temptation.

This approach, often referred to as "exposure therapy" in psychology, works because it gradually desensitises you to temptation while building your confidence in your ability to resist. Think of it as dipping your toes in the water before diving in. You might start by keeping a small piece of chocolate in your desk drawer, allowing yourself to have it only after completing a specific task. As you get more comfortable with this level of control, you can increase the challenge by keeping a whole bar of chocolate nearby or extending the time between indulgences.

The Importance of Consistency and Gradual Progression

The key here is consistency and gradual progression. Do not expect to go from eating a whole pack of biscuits every day to completely abstaining overnight. Such drastic changes often lead to rebound effects and feelings of deprivation, undermining your efforts. Instead, focus on small, sustainable changes that you can maintain over time.

Setting Clear Goals

Next, establishing clear goals is essential. Imagine being in a maze without knowing where the exit is—frustrating, right? Having well-defined, achievable goals acts as your map and compass in such scenarios. They provide direction and purpose. When your goals are specific and measurable, they become motivational anchors during tough times. Instead of saying, "I want to eat healthier," specify your goal: "I will eat two servings of vegetables with each meal." This makes the objective tangible and trackable, offering a structured path forward.

The power of specific, measurable goals lies in their ability to transform vague intentions into concrete actions. When you set a goal like "I will exercise for 30 minutes, three times a week," you are not just stating a desire; you are creating a plan. This specificity makes it easier to track progress and celebrate successes, no matter how small. Moreover, well-defined goals help you stay motivated when willpower starts to flag. On days when you are tempted to skip your workout, having a clear goal reminds you of your commitment. It is not just about immediate action; it is about staying true to your long-term vision for yourself.

The Role of Self-Reflection

Regular self-reflection is a crucial part of the journey. We are often taught to learn from the past, and this practice does precisely that. It is like looking back at a road trip to see which paths were scenic and which led to dead ends. By regularly assessing your choices and motivations, you gain insights into why some decisions were better than others. This kind of introspection reinforces your commitment to healthier decision-making.

Set aside time each week to review your successes and missteps. Ask yourself questions like, "Why did I choose this?" or "What motivated me?" Understanding these factors helps identify behavioural patterns, allowing you to adjust strategies moving forward. Recognising past failures is not about dwelling on them; it is about learning from them.

Self-reflection can take many forms. You might keep a journal, have regular check-ins with an accountability partner, or spend a few quiet minutes at the end of each day reviewing your choices. The key is to approach this practice with curiosity rather than judgment. Instead of berating yourself for slipups, try to understand the circumstances that led to them. Were you particularly stressed that day? Did you skip a meal and end up overly hungry? By identifying these triggers, you can develop strategies to handle similar situations more effectively in the future.

This practice of self-reflection also builds self-awareness, a crucial component of strong willpower. The more you understand your own patterns, motivations, and triggers, the better equipped you will be to navigate challenging situations.

Practising Self-Compassion

Finally, let us talk about the art of practising self-compassion. Before dismissing it as a fluffy concept, consider this: self-compassion is vital because it allows you to recognise setbacks without beating yourself up. Everyone stumbles on this journey; it is part of being human. Instead of criticising yourself for not sticking to your diet or missing a workout, acknowledge the slipup, understand why it happened, and then move on. Treating yourself kindly in these moments fosters a healthier mindset. The key lies in balancing accountability with acceptance. Setbacks are not signs of failure; they are opportunities for growth.

Self-compassion is not about making excuses or letting yourself off the hook. Rather, it is about treating yourself with the same kindness and understanding you would offer a good friend. If your friend told you they missed a workout, would you berate them and tell them they are a failure? Probably not. You would likely offer words of encouragement and help them plan for next time. That is the approach you should take with yourself.

Practising self-compassion can actually strengthen your willpower. When you are not afraid of harsh self-judgement, you are more likely to acknowledge your mistakes and learn from them. This openness to learning and growth is crucial for developing stronger willpower over time.

The Journey of Willpower Development

Remember, willpower is not an innate, fixed trait. It is a skill that can be developed and strengthened over time with the right strategies and mindset. By gradually exposing yourself to temptations, setting clear and specific goals, regularly reflecting on your choices, and practising self-compassion, you are not just building willpower—you are creating a more resilient, self-aware, and balanced version of yourself.

This journey is not about achieving perfection. It is about progress, learning, and growing. There will be days when your willpower feels unshakeable and others when it seems to have abandoned you entirely. The key is to keep moving forward, armed with these strategies and the understanding that each day is a new opportunity to strengthen your mental muscles.

As you embark on or continue your willpower-strengthening journey, be patient with yourself. Celebrate small victories, learn from setbacks, and keep your eyes on the bigger picture. With time and consistent effort, you will find yourself better equipped to handle life's temptations and challenges, steadily moving toward your goals with a stronger, more resilient will.

Key Takeaways

- Design your surroundings to encourage better choices and minimise temptations.

- Incorporate mindfulness to enhance awareness and improve decision-making processes.

- Use gradual exposure to temptations and clear, measurable goals to strengthen willpower.

- Focus on sustainable changes rather than quick fixes for lasting results.

- Engage with supportive people and environments that foster your commitment to healthy choices.

- Define specific and realistic objectives to provide direction and motivation.

- Regularly assess your choices and be kind to yourself when setbacks occur, using them as learning opportunities.

Chapter 8:

Harnessing Dopamine for Positive Goals

Priya stared at her vision board—a colourful collage of dreams and aspirations gathering dust in the corner of her bedroom. Learning to play the guitar, running a 5K, starting a blog—grand plans that had somehow gotten lost in the daily grind. She sighed, wondering why she could not seem to muster the motivation to tackle these goals.

Just then, her phone buzzed. It was a message from her friend Heather: "Hey, did you see? I finally finished that online course we talked about!"

Priya felt a twinge of envy, quickly followed by curiosity. How did Heather always seem to accomplish her goals while she struggled to even get started? She sent back a congratulatory text and then, on impulse, asked, "What is your secret?"

Heather's response came quickly: "Dopamine, my friend. I have been hacking my brain's reward system!"

Intrigued, Priya called her up. "Okay, spill. What is this about dopamine? Isn't that just about pleasure?"

Heather laughed. "It is so much more than that! Think of dopamine as your brain's personal cheerleader. Every time you accomplish something, even something small, it gives you a little high-five. I have been setting tiny goals and celebrating every win. Before I knew it, I was addicted to progress!"

As Heather explained her strategy of breaking down big goals into smaller, achievable tasks, Priya felt a spark of excitement. She glanced at her neglected guitar in the corner.

"So, if I committed to practising for just 10 minutes a day instead of an hour…"

"Exactly!" Heather exclaimed. "Your brain would reward you for those 10 minutes, making you more likely to do it again tomorrow. It is like building a motivation snowball."

Priya's mind raced with possibilities. Maybe she could apply this to her 5K goal too, starting with just a 5-minute jog around the block. And her blog? Perhaps beginning with a single paragraph each day would get the ball rolling.

As she hung up the phone, Priya felt renewed energy. She grabbed a notepad and began breaking down her goals into bite-sized pieces. For the first time in months, her vision board did not seem like a far-off fantasy but a roadmap of exciting possibilities.

Little did Priya know, she was about to embark on a journey of self-discovery, unlocking the power of her brain's own motivational tool kit. By harnessing the subtle yet powerful influence of dopamine, she was about to transform her approach to goal-setting and personal growth.

And that dusty vision board in the corner? It was about to become the most exciting spot in her room.

Setting and Achieving Short-Term Goals

Let us talk about the power of short-term goals—specifically, SMART goals. These are Specific, Measurable, Achievable, Relevant, and Time-bound. Think of them as your brain's favourite snack: bite-sized and easy to digest, keeping you coming back for more. When you accomplish a SMART goal, it is like your brain takes a sip from a motivation fountain. For instance, instead of saying, "I want to write a book," try, "I will write 500 words a day." This approach helps you rack up small wins, maintaining that steady dopamine flow, which is essential for staying motivated (Atlassian, 2019).

Now, let us unleash the power of visual representation with vision boards—a Pinterest board for your life's dreams. Vision boards stimulate excitement and anticipation. By arranging images and words representing your goals, you are priming your brain to feel like you have already taken the first step. Whether it is a photo of that luxurious holiday spot or a symbol of your dream job, these visuals serve as a constant reminder, keeping your spirits high. It is like having your own motivational museum right at home.

Next, onto daily checklists, the unsung heroes of productivity. Imagine your to-do list as an arcade game, with each task a level you need to beat. Every time you check off a task, it is like hitting the jackpot! This triggers a small rush of dopamine—a mini celebration in your mind. Fun fact: some people even add already completed tasks to their checklist just for that satisfying tick mark. It is all about building momentum. A well-structured checklist helps break down daunting projects into manageable tasks. Suddenly, your monstrous project looks less like Godzilla and more like an adorable kitten. Whether on paper or apps like Todoist, embrace your inner checkbox enthusiast and let that dopamine boost fuel your progress (Dart, 2024).

While feedback mechanisms may not sound as exciting as checklists or vision boards, they are essential for building confidence and commitment. Think of feedback like seasoning in soup—the right amount brings out the best flavours. Start with self-assessment: reflect on what you have done and where you can improve. Constructive criticism might sting initially, but remember, it is like a brutal workout—you may not enjoy it in the moment, but you will be stronger for it. Feedback from others can also reveal blind spots and offer fresh perspectives. Going a step further, keep track of negative feedback to help you avoid repeated pitfalls. Whether it is from coworkers, friends, or mentors, constructive input keeps you balanced and focused.

The key is to maintain a rhythm—a harmonious cycle of planning, doing, assessing, and celebrating. Keep your goals dynamic, and your routines flexible, and, most importantly, leave room for fun. This does not mean everything must be relentlessly goal oriented. Sometimes, simply indulging in something for the joy of it can refresh your drive and creativity.

Maintaining Long-Term Motivation

You have a grand vision for your life and are ready to chase it with the enthusiasm of a dog after a squirrel. But unlike those determined pups, you might quickly find that keeping up that initial burst of motivation over the long haul can be challenging. Let us dive into some strategies to help sustain motivation over time.

First off, review and adjust your goals regularly. Just as your car needs routine maintenance to keep running smoothly, your goals require periodic attention to stay relevant and engaging. Goals can lose their appeal if they are not given a little polish now and then. Adjusting them is not about giving up; it is about keeping things fresh and exciting to ensure that dopamine keeps flowing (Berkman, 2018).

Now, let us talk about building a motivational tribe—your support system. Imagine having a group of cheerleaders who do not just cheer but run alongside you. Assembling a network of motivational partners is like creating your own team of goal-chasers. These people share your journey, and whether it is commiserating over setbacks or celebrating wins, these connections boost dopamine for everyone involved. Social connection is a powerful motivator that amplifies your drive because, let us face it, everything is better with company.

Breaking long-term goals into milestones is another key strategy. Tackling a huge goal all at once can feel as tough as eating a pizza while doing yoga. Instead, slice that goal into manageable pieces. Each milestone completed is a little dopamine boost, reinforcing your progress and giving you regular opportunities for strategic planning.

Next, avoid the trap of monotony. Dopamine loves novelty, much like a child loves sweets. Incorporating variety into your goal activities is crucial for staying interested. If working toward your goal feels like watching paint dry, it is time to shake things up. Try a new workout, switch up your study routine, or approach a problem from a fresh angle. Keeping things interesting not only triggers dopamine but also prevents boredom from setting in—because a bored brain is a demotivated brain.

So why does all this matter? Sustaining motivation is not just about reaching the finish line; it is about enjoying the marathon. Regularly tweaking and reviewing your goals, partnering with motivating friends, breaking big goals into achievable pieces, and adding variety ensures that every step of the journey is as rewarding as the destination itself.

Ultimately, you are turning motivation into a renewable resource. Each accomplishment fuels your desire for the next challenge. With dopamine on your side, you are not merely chasing goals; you are creating a series of personal victories, keeping the adventure exciting and fulfilling over the long term.

Using Dopamine to Boost Productivity

Have you ever heard of the *Pomodoro Technique*? It is a simple yet powerful way to break your work into manageable chunks. Here is how it works: Pick a task, set a timer for 25 minutes, work until the timer rings, and then take a 5-minute break. After four rounds, reward yourself with a longer break. This technique gives your brain regular mini workouts without burning out. And every time you finish a "slice," your brain gets a hit of dopamine, making you feel accomplished and ready for more.

Now, think about your workspace. Imagine it as your personal productivity paradise. Is it cluttered with coffee mugs and scattered papers? A tidy, organised space signals to your brain that it is time to focus, not to relax. Good lighting, a touch of greenery, and maybe some inspiring art can switch your brain into "work mode" faster than you would think. It is amazing how much a clean, inviting space can boost your motivation.

Who says work cannot be fun? One way to get dopamine flowing is to turn tasks into little games. Challenge yourself: Can you finish this report faster than yesterday? How many emails can you clear out in 30 minutes? Can you come up with a more creative solution than last time? This "friendly competition" with yourself keeps your brain engaged, with little dopamine rewards each time you beat your record. It makes even the dullest tasks more exciting.

And let us talk about breaks. They might feel like interruptions, but they are actually essential recharges for your brain. Step outside, do a quick dance or even watch that funny video. These pauses keep dopamine levels from dropping like a sugar crash, making breaks vital to long-term productivity. They are not "wasted" time; they are your brain's pit stops to recharge and refocus.

By using these dopamine-friendly techniques, you are not just working harder; you are making work genuinely enjoyable. The aim is not to turn into a "work robot" but to create a balance where your brain feels both challenged and rewarded. If your workday were a road trip, these techniques are like adding your favourite songs to the playlist. They make the journey fun, and before you know it, you have arrived at your destination with a smile on your face!

Remember, everyone's brain is different. Experiment with these ideas to see what fits your style. Whether it is the Pomodoro Technique, workspace tweaks, or gamifying your tasks, find what lights up your motivation. With a bit of practice, you will be riding that dopamine wave to higher productivity in no time!

Key Takeaways

- Dopamine's role: Dopamine is crucial for fuelling motivation and productivity.
- Set SMART goals: Make objectives Specific, Measurable, Achievable, Relevant, and Time-bound.
- Use checklists: Break down tasks into smaller, dopamine-boosting steps.

- Visualise with vision boards: Keep motivation high by visualising your goals.

- Celebrate small wins: Use short-term accomplishments to sustain long-term motivation.

- Sustain motivation: Build support systems and break big goals into manageable milestones.

- Stay connected: Sharing your journey with others amplifies joy and commitment.

- Boost productivity: Apply these strategies to make every step feel rewarding.

Chapter 9:
Real-Life Success Stories

Shane stood before his laptop, his cursor hovering over the "Enrol Now" button of yet another online course. The flashy website promised to turn him into a coding genius practically overnight. It was a familiar scene—the surge of excitement, the vision of a transformed future, all driven by a rush of dopamine.

But this time was different. Instead of clicking, Shane took a deep breath and closed his laptop. He turned to his desk, where an intimidating textbook lay open. It was not exciting, but it was the real path to his goal: becoming a software developer.

Three months earlier, Shane had stumbled upon an article about dopamine's role in motivation and reward. He realised that his impulse to buy courses was just a shortcut to feeling productive without putting in the actual work. Armed with this insight, he began redirecting his dopamine-seeking behaviour toward actions that truly mattered.

Now, as he settled in for a focused study session, Shane allowed himself a small smile. His bank account was healthier, his inbox less cluttered with abandoned course logins, and, most importantly, he was two months into a consistent learning routine. The real reward? Successfully debugging his first substantial program last week.

Shane's journey is a perfect example of how understanding and harnessing dopamine can lead to meaningful change.

Entrepreneurial Success Driven by Dopamine Control

In the fast-paced world of business, understanding how dopamine—the brain's pleasure and reward chemical—functions can be a game-changer for decision-making and achieving success. Here is how some savvy entrepreneurs harness this knowledge to grow their businesses.

Take, for instance, a startup founder who learned to refocus their dopamine responses. Initially, like many entrepreneurs, they fell victim to "shiny object syndrome"—constantly chasing new ideas and short-term wins. However, after realising this scattered approach was not sustainable, they shifted focus to long-term goals. By doing so, they turned the initial rush of quick successes into a steady drive for sustained growth. Think of it as swapping chips for a hearty meal; both satisfy hunger, but only one truly nourishes. This shift was not just about wanting lasting success; it was about understanding how dopamine was steering them away from what truly mattered.

This founder—let us call her Alison—noticed she was frequently jumping from one project to another without fully seeing anything through to completion, driven by the dopamine hit that came with starting something new. Recognising this pattern, Alison implemented a "90-day rule" for new ideas: each new project had to be thoroughly vetted and aligned with long-term goals before being pursued. This channelled her enthusiasm into more productive achievements, bringing a stronger sense of fulfilment.

Structured routines also played a crucial role in limiting distractions and boosting productivity. Imagine trying to work with constant notifications pinging away—it is like reading a book at a rock concert. By establishing a solid routine, Alison minimised distractions and set specific times for deep work, free from digital interruptions. She implemented a "no phones during work blocks" policy for herself and her team, designating two 30-minute periods each day for checking messages and emails. This improved focus and fostered more thoughtful, strategic communication. Without constant interruptions, the team tackled complex problems more effectively, sparking innovative solutions.

Building a supportive network was another vital component. It is incredible what a group of like-minded individuals can achieve when they hold each other accountable. Alison understood that flying solo was tough, so she sought out peers and mentors who shared her vision. This network provided a safety net through regular check-ins and collaborative projects, reinforcing her commitment to long-term goals. Much like having spotters at the gym, this group ensured she stayed on track and inspired her to keep pushing forward. Alison joined a mastermind group of other tech entrepreneurs who met monthly to discuss challenges, share insights, and set goals. When tempted to abandon a tough project for a new idea, her mastermind partners reminded her of her long-term vision, encouraging her to persevere.

None of this would be sustainable without time for rest and self-care. Constant hustle can lead to burnout faster than an iPhone battery on its last leg. Consciously scheduling downtime helped Alison maintain mental clarity and peak performance. She adopted a strict "no work on weekends" policy and committed to at least 30 minutes of daily exercise, usually first thing in the morning. This routine not only boosted her physical health but also provided a natural dopamine lift, which sustained her energy and creativity throughout the day. By prioritising well-being, she found she was more resilient and better equipped to handle stress.

Through managing their dopamine responses, introducing structured routines, nurturing a supportive network, and valuing rest, entrepreneurs like Alison have crafted a sustainable blueprint for business growth. This approach does not just benefit individual entrepreneurs; it transforms entire organisations, fostering innovative, productive, and ethically sound business practices.

Health Transformations Through Balanced Dopamine Management

Meet Aisha. She was tired of feeling stuck in an unhealthy rut. Like many of us, she would try to eat better, or exercise more but always ended up back where she started. Sound familiar? Aisha learned that our brains have a chemical called dopamine that makes us feel good. It is great when it pushes us to make healthy choices, but it can also trick us into bad habits. Understanding this was Aisha's first step toward getting healthier.

Aisha's journey is one many of us can relate to. She would start a new diet on Monday, full of enthusiasm, only to find herself elbow-deep in a bag of crisps by Wednesday evening. It was not that she lacked willpower; she just did not understand how her brain was working against her. Learning about dopamine was like finding a cheat code in her own mind.

Aisha used to grab a snack whenever she felt down. But she started asking herself, "Am I really hungry, or just bored?" This simple question helped her eat when she needed to, not just when she wanted a mood boost. Instead of saying, "I will lose a stone," Aisha started small. Her first goal? To walk around the block without getting winded. When she did it, she celebrated! These little wins kept her going.

This shift in mindset was crucial. Aisha realised that her previous attempts at getting healthy were doomed from the start because she set unrealistic goals. By breaking things down into smaller, achievable steps, she was able to build momentum. Each time she reached a small goal, her brain got a little dopamine boost, reinforcing the positive behaviour.

Aisha hated the idea of going to the gym, so she tried different things until she found something she liked—Zumba classes! She met new friends there, which made her want to go back. The trick is to find an activity that you enjoy.

The Zumba discovery was a game-changer for Aisha. She went from dreading exercise to looking forward to it. It was not just about the physical activity; it was about the fun, the music, and the social connection. This multifaceted approach to exercise meant that she was getting dopamine hits from various sources: physical exertion, the joy of dancing, and the pleasure of social interaction.

Mindfulness was another tool Aisha found invaluable. At first, she felt silly just sitting and breathing, but she stuck with it. After a few weeks, she noticed she was better at catching herself before stress-eating. She would take a few deep breaths instead of automatically reaching for a snack. This practice helped her become more aware of her triggers and gave her a moment to choose her response rather than just reacting.

Getting her friends and family involved made a big difference. Aisha shared her goals with them. Her sister became her workout partner, and her best friend would text to check if she had eaten her veggies. Having people cheer you on can make a world of difference!

This support system was crucial for Aisha. On days when her motivation was low, knowing that her sister was waiting for her at Zumba class got her out the door. Her friend's veggie check-ins became a fun daily ritual, and soon Aisha was sending similar encouraging messages to other friends. This network of support created a positive feedback loop, where everyone was motivating each other to make healthier choices.

Some days, Aisha did not feel like exercising, or she ate too much cake. Instead of beating herself up, she would say, "Tomorrow is a new day." Being kind to yourself helps you stick with it. This self-compassion was a vital part of Aisha's journey. She realised that perfection was not the goal; consistency was. By forgiving herself for slipups, she was able to get back on track quickly instead of spiralling into guilt and unhealthy behaviours.

The great thing about Aisha's story? She did not just lose weight. She learned how to handle stress better, made new friends, and felt prouder of herself. She figured out that getting healthy is not about crash diets or working out until you drop; it is about small, everyday choices that add up over time.

As Aisha continued her journey, she noticed changes that went beyond the number on the scale. She slept better at night, had more energy during the day, and felt more confident in social situations. Her improved health even reflected in her work life—she found herself more focused and productive.

One day, Aisha realised she had not thought about her weight in weeks. She was too busy enjoying her Zumba classes, trying out new healthy recipes with friends, and planning a hiking trip with her sister. Getting healthy had stopped being a chore and had become a natural, enjoyable part of her life.

Aisha's journey shows us that anyone can make healthy changes. It is not always easy, but with tricks to outsmart our brains, support from others, and a lot of patience, we can all become healthier, happier versions of ourselves. Remember, it is not about being perfect; it is about being a little better each day.

What made Aisha's approach work was its holistic nature. She did not just focus on diet and exercise; she addressed the psychological aspects of her health too. By understanding her brain's reward system, building a supportive community, practising mindfulness, and cultivating self-compassion, Aisha created a sustainable lifestyle change.

Her story reminds us that health is not a destination but a journey. It is not about reaching a certain weight or fitting into a particular size; it is about feeling good in your body, having energy for the things you love, and building habits that support your well-being in the long term.

So, next time you are tempted to start a crash diet or buy an expensive gym membership you will never use, remember Aisha's story. Start small, be kind to yourself, find activities you enjoy, and surround yourself with supportive people. Your brain's reward system can work for you instead of against you. With patience and persistence, you too can create lasting, positive changes in your health and life.

Reversing Addictions with Dopamine Understanding

Let us start by looking at what drives addictive behaviours. Often, people turn to substances to cope with stress or escape reality, and that initial dopamine rush hooks the brain, reinforcing the cycle. Recognising these triggers is the first step toward developing healthier coping mechanisms. Imagine feeling stressed, and instead of reaching for a drink or a cigarette, you take up painting or running activities that bring a sense of achievement and pleasure, minus the hangover or hacking cough!

Replacing harmful habits with positive activities is not only about quitting the bad stuff; it is about enriching life with the good stuff that makes it feel vibrant and whole. Think of it as swapping junk food for a gourmet meal: both fill your stomach, but one has far better long-term benefits. By finding new sources of pleasure, you reprogram your brain to associate that dopamine boost with healthier choices.

Being around supportive people and finding a like-minded community can also help immensely. Joining groups like yoga classes, book clubs, or gardening groups offers alternative sources of dopamine. Humans are social beings, and being part of a group provides a sense of belonging and encouragement that is more uplifting than any substance could provide. Bonding over shared interests can lift your spirits in ways that last far longer.

Mindfulness and journalling are also powerful tools for overcoming addiction. Imagine becoming more aware of what is happening in your mind, jotting down your thoughts, reflections, and dreams. You start to see patterns—what triggers your cravings and what helps you resist them. Mindfulness practices like meditation enhance self-awareness, making it easier to pause when faced with temptation.

Mindfulness does not stop at self-awareness; it is also a tool for regulating emotions. By tuning into your emotions, you can choose how to react rather than acting impulsively. Journalling, on the other hand, can feel like having a personal therapist on call. It is a space to spill everything—fears, triumphs, setbacks—and find clarity through the chaos. Both practices encourage proactive choices, helping you manage triggers more effectively.

Neuroscience supports these approaches. Self-regulation theory emphasises setting standards, maintaining motivation, and tracking progress (Schuman-Olivier et al., 2020). These processes are crucial for behaviour change, serving as a guide to avoiding addictive paths. Mindfulness enhances control over actions through attention regulation and inhibition switching, helping to maintain a balance between healthy and unhealthy patterns.

For those dealing with co-occurring disorders, such as addiction and mental health issues, alternative methods like these can be invaluable (American Addiction Centers, 2019). Since drugs often provide temporary relief for untreated mental illnesses, adopting strategies that build resilience can profoundly impact recovery.

Academic Achievements Through Disciplined Dopamine Use

In the bustling world of academia, success is not solely about hitting the books; it also hinges on managing our brain chemistry. Dopamine plays a crucial role in those feel-good moments when you finally solve a tricky math problem or complete an all-nighter essay. For students aiming to maximise their academic performance, understanding and regulating dopamine can be a game changer.

Developing effective study habits involves maximising focus and evaluating learning environments to enhance outcomes. Imagine trying to study in a noisy cafeteria—not ideal, right?

The environment can either support or hinder your learning capabilities. It is also important to create conditions that keep dopamine levels balanced. Engaging with the material in manageable chunks helps maintain concentration without overwhelming the brain. This strategy allows students to avoid burnout while ensuring they absorb all the necessary information.

Procrastination is a common struggle for students. What if the solution lies in how you manage dopamine? Techniques like breaking tasks into small, digestible parts paired with a reward system can help combat this issue. For example, you might tell yourself, "I will study this chapter for 30 minutes, then watch an episode of my favourite show." This balance between instant gratification and long-term achievement keeps dopamine levels healthy and motivates continuous progress (Haikal, 2021).

Every student is familiar with distractions lurking around every corner—whether it is social media's siren call or the endless allure of streaming services. Enter active learning approaches. Incorporating interactive elements like flashcards or group discussions keeps students engaged, counteracting the pitfalls of passive consumption. Adjusting the learning environment is also crucial for maintaining motivation. A room adorned with motivational quotes or organised study materials can nudge the brain into a productive state.

Let us explore how some exceptionally successful students manage to get things done without losing their minds. It is not magic; they have simply learned to make their brain's "feel-good" system work for them instead of against them. Instead of scrolling on their phones when they should be studying, they stick to a schedule that includes work sessions followed by short breaks for enjoyable activities.

This strategy feels like giving yourself a little treat for completing your tasks—something that many top students swear by.

Interestingly, spending excessive time on apps like TikTok when trying to avoid work can actually worsen your mood. While it may seem like a good way to relax, it can lead to increased stress and feelings of discouragement. So, it is worth considering before diving into an endless scroll session.

Here is a helpful trick: pair something you love with something you need to do. For instance, if you enjoy listening to your favourite podcast, save it for when you are doing laundry or cleaning your room. This way, you will look forward to tackling those jobs!

Do not overlook your study space. It does not need to be extravagant, but maintaining a tidy and well-lit area can significantly enhance your focus. You would be surprised at how much easier it is to concentrate when your desk is organised. The big secret? It is all about creating small, positive habits. These habits help keep your brain happy and motivated, making it easier to stay on track with your studies. As you practise these strategies, you will find yourself genuinely looking forward to completing your work.

Key Takeaways

- Dopamine management: Transform your brain's reward system from a source of distraction into a powerful tool for personal growth and goal achievement.

- Success strategies: Redirect feel-good impulses toward healthier routines, build supportive networks, practice mindfulness, and prioritise long-term solutions over quick fixes.

- Widespread applications: From entrepreneurship and weight loss to addiction recovery and academic success, mastering dopamine can lead to significant improvements across various aspects of life.

Chapter 10:

Managing Dopamine:

Crafting a Balanced Life

James stared at the clock: 2:37 a.m. His bloodshot eyes darted back to the laptop screen, where Netflix helpfully asked, "Are you still watching?" For the fifth time that night. "Just one more episode," he muttered, reaching for his third energy drink. He knew he had a big presentation at work in... six hours. Yet here he was, deep into a series binge that had started as "just 30 minutes to unwind."

As the next episode loaded, James's phone lit up with a notification. A friend had liked his latest social media post. Without thinking, he grabbed his phone and soon found himself scrolling mindlessly through his feed.

Somewhere in the fog of his tired brain, James remembered reading about dopamine and its effects on behaviour. He had laughed it off then, thinking, "I have my habits under control." Now, as dawn approached and his presentation loomed, the irony was not lost on him.

James's night was a perfect storm of dopamine-driven decisions: the addictive pull of "just one more" episode, the allure of sugary caffeinated drinks, and the siren song of social media validation. Each choice gave him a little hit of pleasure, but at what cost?

As he finally shut his laptop and collapsed into bed, James made a promise to himself: tomorrow, he would learn how to wrangle this dopamine thing. After his presentation. And maybe after just one more episode...

James's late-night adventure is a familiar tale in our dopamine-drenched world. In this chapter, we will explore how to dance with dopamine without letting it lead you off a cliff. From understanding why your brain loves that "new message" ping to learning tricks to make boring tasks more appealing, we are about to embark on a journey to master the art of dopamine management.

Creating Healthy Habits

Do not worry; you are not at the mercy of your brain chemistry. With a few simple tweaks to your daily routine, you can take control of your dopamine levels. This means more consistent energy, better focus, and feeling good without constantly chasing the next big thrill. Let us dive into some practical strategies to help you manage your dopamine levels effectively.

Exercise is a natural mood booster. It is not about becoming a gym rat or running marathons; even a brisk walk around the block or a dance party in your living room counts. When you move, your brain releases feel-good chemicals, including dopamine. It is like giving yourself a high-five from the inside out. Plus, regular exercise can help you focus better and feel more motivated in other areas of your life. So, the next time you are feeling low or stressed, try putting on your favourite tunes and dancing them out for a few minutes.

For example, Jane, a busy marketing executive, found herself constantly drained and reaching for her phone for quick dopamine hits. She decided to start her day with a 15-minute yoga session. Within a week, she noticed she had more energy throughout the day and was less tempted to scroll through social media during her breaks. The key is consistency—short bursts of activity can make a big difference over time.

We have talked about mindfulness before. It is like hitting the pause button on life's chaos. You do not need to sit cross-legged and chant "Om" (unless you want to). Just take a few deep breaths before responding to a stressful email, or really focus on the taste of your morning coffee. These little moments of awareness can help you make better choices throughout the day. Instead of automatically reaching for your phone when bored, you might notice the urge and choose to do something else instead.

Consider Tom, a student who found himself constantly distracted during study sessions. He started practising mindfulness by using the Pomodoro Technique—25 minutes of focused work followed by a 5-minute break. During his breaks, instead of immediately checking his phone, he would take a moment to stretch and breathe deeply. This simple practice helped him stay more focused during study sessions and reduced his overall screen time.

Think of sleep as your brain's cleaning crew. It sweeps away the day's junk and gets you ready for tomorrow. Try to stick to a regular sleep schedule, even on weekends. As for food, you do not need to go on a crazy diet. Just aim for a mix of fruits, vegetables, whole grains, and proteins. These foods provide your brain with the building blocks it needs to function properly. Small changes, like swapping out your afternoon sugar filled, fizzy drink for water or herbal tea, can make a big difference over time.

Mel, a night owl who often found herself scrolling through social media until the early hours, decided to establish a bedtime routine. She set a "phone curfew" an hour before bed, replacing screen time with reading a book. She also started having a small snack of nuts and berries in the evening instead of sugary treats. After a few weeks, she noticed she was falling asleep more easily and waking up feeling more refreshed.

Humans are like plants—we need the right environment to thrive. Surrounding yourself with positive people is like giving yourself good soil and sunlight. Join a club, volunteer, or just call a friend for a chat. These connections provide a natural dopamine boost without the need to scroll through social media for likes. Plus, doing activities with others (like a workout class or a cooking group) can make healthy habits more fun and easier to stick to.

Ian, who worked from home, realised he was feeling increasingly isolated and turning to online shopping for quick dopamine hits. He decided to join a local hiking group that met every weekend. Not only did he benefit from exercise and nature, but he also formed new friendships. He found that the anticipation of these weekly hikes and the social interaction provided a more sustainable source of dopamine than his online shopping habit.

Engage in activities that make you lose track of time in a good way. Maybe it is painting, gardening, or solving puzzles. These "flow" states are natural dopamine boosters that leave you feeling satisfied and fulfilled. For instance, Emma, a busy mother of two, rediscovered her love for knitting. She found that spending an hour in the evening working on a project helped her relax and reduced her urge to mindlessly watch TV or scroll through social media.

End each day by thinking of three things you are grateful for. It could be as simple as "I am thankful for that delicious sandwich I had for lunch." This practice helps train your brain to notice the good stuff, providing little dopamine boosts throughout the day. John, a software developer prone to negative self-talk, started a gratitude journal. After a month, he noticed he was more optimistic and better able to handle work stress without resorting to stress-eating or excessive caffeine intake.

Our phones and computers are designed to keep us hooked. Try setting specific times to check social media or emails instead of constantly peeking at notifications. Use apps that limit your screen time if needed. Replace some of that scrolling time with a hobby or face-to-face conversation. Rachel, a social media manager, found it challenging to disconnect from work. She decided to use app-blocking software during her off-hours and replaced her morning social media check with a 10-minute stretching routine. She soon found she was starting her days feeling more centred and less anxious.

Nature is a fantastic dopamine regulator. Even a few minutes in a park or garden can help reset your brain. If you can, try to get some sunlight early in the day—it helps regulate your sleep-wake cycle. David, an office worker, started taking his lunch breaks in a nearby park instead of at his desk. He found that this midday nature break helped him feel more energised and focused for the rest of the afternoon, reducing his reliance on sugary snacks and excessive coffee for a pick-me-up.

Nobody is perfect. If you slip up and binge-watch an entire season in one night, do not beat yourself up. Acknowledge it, learn from it, and move on. Treating yourself with compassion is key to maintaining balanced dopamine levels in the long run. Maria, a recovering social media addict, had a day when she fell back into old habits and spent hours scrolling. Instead of berating herself, she reflected on what triggered the behaviour and made a plan to handle similar situations better in the future. This compassionate approach helped her maintain her overall progress without getting discouraged by temporary setbacks.

By incorporating these practical tips into your daily life, you can start managing your dopamine levels more effectively. It is not about eliminating pleasure from your life; it is about finding sustainable ways to feel good and stay motivated. Start small, be consistent, and soon you will notice positive changes in how you feel and function.

Remember, the goal is not to never experience a dopamine rush from social media or other quick fixes. It is about creating a balanced life where these are not your primary sources of satisfaction. By diversifying your dopamine sources through activities like exercise, mindfulness, healthy relationships, and engaging hobbies, you are creating a more stable and sustainable sense of well-being.

Think of it like creating a diverse investment portfolio for your brain. Just as you would not put all your money into a single, volatile stock, you should not rely on a single source for all your feel-good brain chemicals. By spreading out your dopamine-inducing activities, you are less likely to experience extreme highs and lows, and more likely to maintain a steady state of contentment and motivation.

As you implement these changes, pay attention to how you feel. You might notice that you are less prone to mood swings, more able to focus on tasks, and generally more satisfied with your day-to-day life. You may find yourself less tempted by impulsive behaviours and better able to work toward long-term goals.

Remember, change does not happen overnight. Be patient with yourself as you build these new habits. Celebrate small victories along the way. Maybe you went a whole day without checking social media, or you chose to go for a walk instead of watching another episode of your favourite show. These small choices add up over time, gradually reshaping your brain's reward system to favour more balanced and sustainable sources of dopamine.

By taking control of your dopamine levels, you are not just improving your mood; you are setting yourself up for a more balanced, fulfilling life. You are training your brain to find joy in the simple things, to be more present in your daily experiences, and to derive satisfaction from personal growth and meaningful connections. This is the path to sustainable happiness and well-being, far more rewarding than the fleeting highs of constant dopamine chasing.

The "Dopamine-Friendly Day Planner"

Purpose: This activity helps you structure your day to balance dopamine levels by combining small rewards with productive tasks.

Materials Needed:

- A notebook or planner
- Coloured pens or markers

Step 1: Morning Mapping (5 minutes)

Start your day by writing down 3-5 tasks you need to accomplish. Next to each task, draw a small box.

Step 2: Reward Brainstorm (5 minutes)

List 5-10 small, healthy activities you enjoy.

Examples:

- Taking a 10-minute walk
- Listening to a favourite song
- Calling a friend for a quick chat
- Doing a quick stretching routine
- Reading a chapter of a book

Step 3: Task-Reward Pairing (5 minutes)

For each task, choose a reward from your list and write it next to the task's checkbox.

Step 4: Time Blocking (5 minutes)

Assign realistic time blocks for each task-reward pair.

For example:

- 9:00-10:30AM:

Work on project report ☐
Reward: 10-minute walk

- 11:00-12:00PM:

Answer emails ☐
Reward: Listen to a favourite song

Step 5: Execution

As you complete each task, check the box and immediately do the associated reward activity. This reinforces the connection between productivity and positive feelings.

Step 6: Evening Reflection (5 minutes)

At the end of the day, review your planner. Circle the task-reward pairs that felt most satisfying. Use this information to plan better for tomorrow.

Tips:

- Start small. Do not overwhelm yourself with too many tasks.

- Be flexible. If a task takes longer than expected, adjust your schedule.

- Experiment with different rewards to see what works best for you.

- Consider using a habit-tracking app to complement this activity.

By consistently using this planner, you are training your brain to associate productive tasks with positive feelings, creating a more balanced dopamine response throughout your day.

Key Takeaways

- Our brains constantly seek dopamine-inducing rewards, which can sometimes lead to impulsive decisions.

- Understanding the effects of dopamine empowers us to make smarter choices.

- The goal is to find balance: using dopamine as motivation without letting it control us.

- Managing dopamine involves: Setting boundaries with technology

- Practicing mindfulness and savouring peaceful moments
- Embracing healthier routines for long-term happiness

Conclusion

Let us dive into the journey of understanding dopamine and how it affects our daily lives. Imagine you have just finished reading a book that opens your eyes to the sneaky ways your brain works. It is not just about resisting that tempting doughnut at the coffee shop anymore; it is about getting to know yourself better—like finally figuring out why you cannot stop scrolling through social media when you should be sleeping.

Dopamine is like that friend who always suggests going out for "just one drink" on a work night. It promises fun and excitement but conveniently forgets to mention the hangover the morning after. Now that you understand this little brain chemical better, it is almost like having x-ray vision that lets you see through the shiny wrapper of instant gratification to what is really inside.

Think about the last time you binged a TV series. Remember that "just one more episode" feeling? That is dopamine talking. It is not evil; it is just doing its job, trying to make you feel good. But now you know its tricks. Next time you are about to click "Next Episode" at 2 a.m., you might pause and think, "Is this really what I want, or is dopamine pulling a fast one on me?"

Knowing about dopamine is just the first step. It is like getting a shiny new toolbox—great to have, but not much use if you leave it in the garage. So let us talk about putting this knowledge to work in your everyday life.

Maybe tomorrow morning, instead of reaching for your phone the second you wake up, take a deep breath and stretch first. It might feel weird at first, like wearing shoes on the wrong feet, but stick with it. Each time you make a choice that is good for you in the long run—even if it is tiny—you are rewiring your brain. You are teaching it to enjoy the slow burn of long-term satisfaction over the quick hit of instant pleasure.

A fun way to think about it is to imagine you are the director of a movie called "Your Life." Dopamine is like that enthusiastic but sometimes misguided assistant always pitching wild ideas. "Let us have the main character eat an entire pizza at midnight!" they might suggest. Before, you might have gone along with it; now, you can smile, say, "Interesting idea," and choose a script that better fits your life's story.

Remember, this is not about becoming a robot who never has fun. It is about finding a balance. Maybe you decide to have that piece of cake at the party, but you really savour it instead of mindlessly munching. Or you watch that extra episode, but you make a deal with yourself to go to bed early the next night. It is all about making conscious choices rather than letting autopilot—or, should we say, dopamine-pilot—steer your life.

As you practise this new awareness, you will start noticing changes. It is like watching a garden grow. At first, nothing seems different, but one day you realise you are naturally reaching for an apple instead of crisps or turning off Netflix without a struggle to dive into that project you have been meaning to start. These are your flowers blooming—proof that your efforts are paying off.

Now, let us talk about the bumps in the road because they are definitely coming. There will be days when you cave and buy that gadget you do not need or spend hours on a social media binge. That is totally normal. Change is not a straight line; it is more like a squiggly doodle. The important thing is not to let these moments derail you.

Instead of beating yourself up, get curious. Ask yourself, "What was going on that made me vulnerable to that dopamine hit?" Maybe you were stressed, tired, or lonely. Understanding your triggers is like having a weather forecast for your moods—it helps you prepare for the storms.

One powerful tool in your new dopamine-savvy tool kit is community. Humans are social creatures, and we are stronger together. Find your tribe—people who are also trying to make thoughtful choices in their lives. This could be a friend you meet for coffee to chat about your goals, an online forum where you share victories and setbacks, or a family member you check in with regularly. When you are surrounded by people who understand what you are trying to do, it is like having a cheering squad for your brain.

Picture this: You are at dinner with friends, and someone mentions how they resisted buying the latest smartphone model, choosing to put that money toward a savings goal instead. Suddenly, the conversation lights up. Others chime in with their own stories of choosing long-term satisfaction over quick thrills. There is laughter, there is support, and there is a sense that you are all in this together. This kind of sharing does double duty—it reinforces your own good habits and inspires others.

As you move forward with your new understanding of dopamine, keep your sense of humour handy. Life is too short to take everything seriously. So, when you find yourself elbow-deep in a crisp packet after swearing off junk food, laugh it off. Dust off the crumbs and get back on track. Your ability to bounce back with a smile is just as important as your ability to resist temptation in the first place.

Here is a practical tip: start a "dopamine diary." Each day, jot down one situation where you recognised dopamine's influence and made a conscious choice. Maybe you opted for a walk instead of scrolling through your phone or chose to save money instead of buying something on impulse. Over time, this diary becomes a record of your growth—a reminder of how far you have come.

Remember, the goal is not to control every aspect of your life with an iron fist. It is about becoming aware of the invisible strings that often guide our actions and learning to gently redirect them. Think of it like learning to dance with dopamine instead of being pushed around by it.

As you continue on this path, you will likely find that your definition of "reward" starts to shift. Things that used to give you a quick high might lose their appeal, replaced by the deep satisfaction of aligning your actions with your values. That promotion at work you earned through consistent effort and the genuine connections you have built by being present with friends instead of distracted by your phone—these become your new sources of joy.

Do not forget to celebrate your progress, no matter how small. Did you make it through a day without impulsive purchases? That is worth a happy dance in your living room. Did you choose a book over binge-watching?

These celebrations serve a dual purpose—they acknowledge your efforts and give you a healthy dose of dopamine that reinforces your good habits.

As you wrap up this chapter of your journey, remember that this is just the beginning. Your understanding of dopamine and its effects on your choices is a powerful tool, but like any tool, it gets better with use. Keep questioning, keep learning, and keep growing. Your future self—the one making confident decisions, pursuing meaningful goals, and finding joy in the journey—is cheering you on.

So, here's to you, armed with knowledge and ready to write the next chapter of your life. It is a story of small victories, occasional setbacks, and continuous growth. A story where you are not just a character being pushed along by unseen forces but the author making conscious choices.

References

Adinoff, B. (2004, November). *Neurobiologic processes in drug reward and addiction.* Harvard Review of Psychiatry. https://doi.org/10.1080/10673220490910844

Atlassian. (2019, April 23). *How checklists train your brain to be more productive and goal-oriented.* Work Life by Atlassian. https://www.atlassian.com/blog/productivity/the-psychology-of-checklists-why-setting-small-goals-motivates-us-to-accomplish-bigger-things

Belujon, P., & Grace, A. A. (2017, June 29). *Dopamine system dysregulation in major depressive disorders.* International Journal of Neuropsychopharmacology. https://doi.org/10.1093/ijnp/pyx056

Berkman, E. T. (2018, March). *The neuroscience of goals and behavior change.* Consulting Psychology Journal: Practice and Research. https://doi.org/10.1037/cpb0000094

Bromberg-Martin, E. S., Matsumoto, M., & Hikosaka, O. (2010, December 9). *Dopamine in motivational control: Rewarding, aversive, and alerting.* Neuron. https://doi.org/10.1016/j.neuron.2010.11.022

Burns, H. (2024, August 30). *The 7 best habits for improving self-discipline.* New Trader U. https://www.newtraderu.com/2024/08/30/10-simple-ways-to-develop-self-discipline-according-to-psychology/

Chowdhury, M. R. (2019, April 9). *The neuroscience of gratitude and effects on the brain.* PositivePsychology.com. https://positivepsychology.com/neuroscience-of-gratitude/

Cleveland Clinic. (2022, March 23). *Dopamine.* Cleveland Clinic. https://my.clevelandclinic.org/health/articles/22581-dopamine

Dagdeviren, O. (2019). *Hacking your brain to use dopamine for success.* Medium. https://medium.com/@ozandagdeviren/hacking-your-brain-to-use-dopamine-for-success-ed2d352b4874

De Posada, J. (n.d.). *Don't eat the marshmallow yet! The secret to sweet success in work and life.* https://www.bookey.app/book/don't-eat-the-marshmallow-yet!-the-secret-to-sweet-success-in-work-and-life

Dowling, L. (2023, October 23). *Exploring the neurological roots of consumer behavior.* Pathmonk. https://pathmonk.com/exploring-the-neurological-roots-of-consumer-behavior/

Freels, T. G., Gabriel, D. B. K., Lester, D. B., & Simon, N. W. (2020, January 1). *Risky decision-making predicts dopamine release dynamics in nucleus accumbens shell.* Neuropsychopharmacology. https://doi.org/10.1038/s41386-019-0527-0

Haynes, T. (2018, May 1). *Dopamine, smartphones & you: A battle for your time*. Science in the News; Harvard University. https://sitn.hms.harvard.edu/flash/2018/dopamine-smartphones-battle-time/

Huberman, A. (2022, October 6). *Tools to manage dopamine and improve motivation & drive* - Huberman Lab. https://www.hubermanlab.com/newsletter/tools-to-manage-dopamine-and-improve-motivation-and-drive

Juárez Olguín, H., Calderón Guzmán, D., Hernández García, E., & Barragán Mejía, G. (2016). *The role of dopamine and its dysfunction as a consequence of oxidative stress*. Oxidative Medicine and Cellular Longevity. https://doi.org/10.1155/2016/9730467

Kirk, U., Gu, X., Sharp, C., Hula, A., Fonagy, P., & Montague, P. R. (2016, September). *Mindfulness training increases cooperative decision making in economic exchanges: Evidence from fMRI*. NeuroImage. https://doi.org/10.1016/j.neuroimage.2016.05.075

Lambrecht, A. (n.d.). *I tried a "dopamine detox" to boost my productivity. Here's how it worked and why I'll keep doing it*. Business Insider. https://www.businessinsider.com/i-tried-dopamine-restricting-for-procrastination-motivation-productivity-strategy-2022-6

LaVine, R. (2023, August 12). *Dopamine: how to regulate it naturally (Why it's linked to pleasure)*. Science of People. https://www.scienceofpeople.com/dopamine/

Liang, P., Jiang, H., Wang, H., & Tang, J. (2024, January 11). *Mindfulness and impulsive behavior: exploring the mediating roles of self-reflection and coping effectiveness among high-level athletes in Central China.* Frontiers in Psychology. https://doi.org/10.3389/fpsyg.2024.1304901

Martín-Rodríguez, A., Gostian-Ropotin, L. A., Beltrán-Velasco, A. I., Belando-Pedreño, N., Simón, J. A., López-Mora, C., Navarro-Jiménez, E., Tornero-Aguilera, J. F., & Clemente-Suárez, V. J. (2024, January 1). *Sporting mind: The interplay of physical activity and psychological health.* Sports. https://doi.org/10.3390/sports12010037

McLean Hospital. (2024, March 29). *The social dilemma: social media and your mental health.* McLean Hospital. https://www.mcleanhospital.org/essential/it-or-not-social-medias-affecting-your-mental-health

McLachlan, S. (2021, December 22). *The science of habit: How to rewire your brain.* Healthline. https://www.healthline.com/health/the-science-of-habit

Md Najmul Hossain, Lee, J., Choi, H., Kwak, Y.-S., & Kim, J. (2024, June 30). *The impact of exercise on depression: how moving makes your brain and body feel better.* Physical Activity and Nutrition. https://doi.org/10.20463/pan.2024.0015

Mendelsohn, A. I. (2019, June 1). *Creatures of habit: The neuroscience of habit and purposeful behavior.* Biological Psychiatry. https://doi.org/10.1016/j.biopsych.2019.03.978

Miles, M. (2023, April 28). *Leverage your decision-making style to make better choices.* www.betterup.com. https://www.betterup.com/blog/decision-making-style

Miller, S. (2022, June 2). *The addictiveness of social media: How teens get hooked.* Jefferson Health. https://www.jeffersonhealth.org/your-health/living-well/the-addictiveness-of-social-media-how-teens-get-hookedKirk, U., Gu, X., Sharp, C., Hula, A., Fonagy, P., & Montague, P. R. (2016, September). Mindfulness training increases cooperative decision making in economic exchanges: Evidence from fMRI. NeuroImage. https://doi.org/10.1016/j.neuroimage.2016.05.075

Paul, J. (2024, June 20). *How to practice delayed gratification to achieve your goals - Dr. Magie Cook.* https://magiecook.com/blog/how-to-practice-delayed-gratification-to-achieve-your-goals/

Poisson, C. L., Engel, L., & Saunders, B. T. (2021, November 9). *Dopamine circuit mechanisms of addiction-like behaviors.* Frontiers in Neural Circuits. https://doi.org/10.3389/fncir.2021.752420

Prieur, J. (2022, March 11). *13 ways to create a positive learning environment in your classroom.* Prodigy Game. https://www.prodigygame.com/main-en/blog/positive-learning-environment/

ProofHub. (2019, February 22). *The Pomodoro technique to kick your productivity up a notch.* ProofHub Blog. https://blog.proofhub.com/the-pomodoro-technique-to-kick-your-productivity-up-a-notch-62982e983c7d

Radtke, D. (2023). *Understanding the fluctuating nature of fatigue.* Brain Facts. https://www.brainfacts.org/thinking-sensing-and-behaving/thinking-and-awareness/2023/how-fatigue-affects-our-decisions-and-desires--041823

Ralph, K. (2024, January 31). *Habit stacking: How to hack your habit loop for lasting change.* Chiropractic Life. https://chiropracticlife.com.au/blog/habit-stacking-how-to-hack-your-habit-loop-for-lasting-change/

Rogers, R. D. (2010, September 29). *The roles of dopamine and serotonin in decision making: Evidence from pharmacological experiments in humans.* Neuropsychopharmacology. https://doi.org/10.1038/npp.2010.165

Rogowska, A. M., & Cincio, A. (2024, January 1). *Procrastination mediates the relationship between problematic TikTok use and depression among young adults.* Journal of Clinical Medicine. https://doi.org/10.3390/jcm13051247

Ryan, K. (2016, September 19). *Five ways junk food changes your brain.* www.rmit.edu.au. https://www.rmit.edu.au/news/all-news/2016/sep/five-ways-junk-food-changes-your-brain

Schuman-Olivier, Z., Trombka, M., Lovas, D. A., Brewer, J. A., Vago, D. R., Gawande, R., Dunne, J. P., Lazar, S. W., Loucks, E. B., & Fulwiler, C. (2020). Mindfulness and behavior change. Harvard Review of Psychiatry. https://doi.org/10.1097/HRP.0000000000000277

Simon, N. W., Montgomery, K. S., Beas, B. S., Mitchell, M. R., LaSarge, C. L., Mendez, I. A., Banuelos, C., Vokes, C. M., Taylor, A. B., Haberman, R. P., Bizon, J. L., & Setlow, B. (2011, November 30). *Dopaminergic modulation of risky decision-making.* Journal of Neuroscience. https://doi.org/10.1523/jneurosci.3772-11.2011

Smith, J. A. (2024, March 28). *Dopamine in a digital age.* The Dawn Wellness Centre and Rehab Thailand. https://thedawnrehab.com/blog/dopamine-in-a-digital-age/

Volkow, N. D., Michaelides, M., & Baler, R. (2019, September 11). *The neuroscience of drug reward and addiction.* Physiological Reviews. https://doi.org/10.1152/physrev.00014.2018

Volkow, N. D., Wang, G.-J., Fowler, J. S., Tomasi, D., Telang, F., & Baler, R. (2010, August 17). *Addiction: Decreased reward sensitivity and increased expectation sensitivity conspire to overwhelm the brain's control circuit.* BioEssays. https://doi.org/10.1002/bies.201000042

Walton, M. E., & Bouret, S. (2019, February). *What is the relationship between dopamine and effort?* Trends in Neurosciences. https://doi.org/10.1016/j.tins.2018.10.001

Waters, J. (2021, August 22). *Constant craving: How digital media turned us all into dopamine addicts.* The Guardian. https://www.theguardian.com/global/2021/aug/22/how-digital-media-turned-us-all-into-dopamine-addicts-and-what-we-can-do-to-break-the-cycle

Zabelina, D. L., Colzato, L., Beeman, M., & Hommel, B. (2016, January 19). *Dopamine and the creative mind: individual differences in creativity are predicted by interactions between dopamine genes DAT and COMT* (A. Antonietti, Ed.). PLOS ONE. https://doi.org/10.1371/journal.pone.0146768

Printed in Great Britain
by Amazon